To:

....

From:

....

Endorsements

"In *Praying Circles Around the Lives of Your Children*, Mark outlines stories and strategies that equip families to love God more and enjoy a sacred, lasting relationship with Him through prayer. I cannot think of a more impactful legacy that a parent can give to a child."

— DR. GARY SMALLEY, AUTHOR OF
THE DNA OF RELATIONSHIPS

"Mark Batterson has done it again! He has challenged and convicted me with the valuable, practical, fun tools to transform my prayer life for my children and grandchildren. I love it! Read this book, tap into the resource and begin today to draw circles around those you love—and some you don't!"

— RUTH GRAHAM, AUTHOR OF *IN
EVERY PEW SITS A BROKEN HEART*

"As parents we know it's important to pray for our kids, but *Praying Circles Around the Lives of Your Children* goes way beyond the that. Packed within its pages are practical helps with vocabulary, a new framework for your prayer methodology, and inspiration that will change your prayer life forever. This book is a powerful tool that needs to be in the hands of every mom and dad."

— SHERRY SURRATT, CEO AND PRESIDENT,
MOPS INTERNATIONAL, AUTHOR OF *JUST LEAD!
FOR WOMEN LEADERS AND BRAVE MOM: FACING
AND OVERCOMING YOUR REAL MOM FEARS*

Praying Circles

Around *the* Lives *of*

Your Children

Mark Batterson

ZONDERVAN®

ZONDERVAN

Praying Circles Around the Lives of Your Children

Copyright © 2014 by Mark Batterson

Requests for information should be addressed to:
Zondervan, *Grand Rapids, Michigan 49530*

ISBN: 978-0-31033-973-1

Published in association with the literary agency of Fedd & Company, Inc., Post Office Box 341973, Austin, TX 78734.

Contents

1. The Greatest Legacy You Can Leave   1
2. The Legend of the Circle Maker   17
3. Seven Prayer Circles   37
4. The 1st Circle: Circling the Promises of God   45
5. The 2nd Circle: Making Prayer Lists   69
6. The 3rd Circle: Creating Prayer Mantras   83
7. The 4th Circle: Praying a Hedge of Protection   103
8. The 5th Circle: Forming Prayer Circles   121
9. The 6th Circle: Praying Through the Bible   141
10. The 7th Circle: Passing On the Blessing   151
11. Teachable Moments   173
12. Holy Complications   185

Notes   195

Bible Versions Cited   199

Chapter 1

The Greatest Legacy
You Can Leave

Only be careful, and watch yourselves closely
so that you do not forget the things your
eyes have seen or let them fade from your
heart as long as you live. Teach them to your
children and to their children after them.

DEUTERONOMY 4:9

I want to be famous in my home.

That is the deepest desire of my heart and the greatest challenge of my life. Parenting our three children is far more difficult—and far more important—than pastoring thousands of people. Compared to parenting, every other challenge is child's play. Being a mom or dad is our single greatest privilege. And while I've never met a mom or dad who disagrees with me on that point, it's easy to end up with inverted priorities. But at the end of the day, *I want those who know me best to respect me most.* That's my family. And that's my definition of success. Of course, it's much easier said than done.

During a recent parenting slump, I facetiously said to my wife, Lora, "I think we'll finally figure out this parenting thing the same day our kids leave home!" The truth is, we'll never figure it out because children are moving targets. Just when you think you have them pegged, they become toddlers or teenagers or twentysomethings, and you're right back to square one. I've come to the conclusion that parenting is not a puzzle to be solved. Parenting is more like a roller coaster you ride for eighteen years with no exit. The relational corkscrews and emotional inversions result in exhilarating highs and nauseating lows. So my advice is simple: buckle up, learn a few lessons along the way, and enjoy the ride.

You will make more mistakes than you care to remember, especially with the guinea pigs we call firstborns. But no matter how many things you get wrong, there is one thing you must get right—and that one thing makes all the difference in the world:

Make sure the heavenly Father hears about your kids every day!

Bad News, Good News, and Great News

Right at the outset, let me give you some bad news, some good news, and some great news about parenting and praying for your children.

The bad news first: *you'll feel like a failure at the end of many, if not most, days.*

There are days you need to take a mulligan. Go to bed, get up the next morning, and start over. There's nothing like a good night's sleep to help you hit the reset button. I realize that isn't a luxury you have if you have a newborn baby, but the same baby you have a tough time getting to sleep will one day be difficult to wake up because they missed curfew the night before. My advice? Take a short nap as often as you can.

I've already revealed my definition of success: *I want those who know me best to respect me most.* That's the dream. But the reality is that I often feel like a complete failure as a father. Some days I even feel like a fraud. It's usually those moments when one of our mini-mes begins to mimic something I don't like about myself. It's a sobering thing when you say, "Don't take that tone with me" and then realize it's the same exact tone you take with them.

Having children is like looking in the mirror on a really bad hair day or looking at old pictures from a fashion season you'd like to forget. Kids keep us humble! Just when you think they've mastered the art of Emily Post etiquette, they'll mortify you by making a passing comment or passing gas at the most inopportune time. Of course, they learned this from you as well. In the infamous words of John Wilmot, "Before I got married, I had six theories about raising children; now I have six children and no theories."[1] Nothing keeps you on your knees or on your toes like parenting.

My parenting ineptitude is epitomized by one shining moment when our oldest son, Parker, was a toddler. He had a fitful night full of tears, and I couldn't understand why. Then he crawled into our room in the middle of the night. I was too tired to take him back to his bed, so I reached down to pull him into ours. That's when I realized why he had been crying—his bare butt was the tip-off that I had forgotten to put a diaper on him when I put him to bed.

It's amazing that our kids even survive our parenting, isn't it?

While we're on the subject, the word *diaper* spelled backward is *repaid*. So apropos!

Just as our children won't fully appreciate the sacrifices we've made for them until they have kids of their own, I think it's impossible to fully appreciate the heavenly Father until you have kids of your own. I have three graduate degrees in theology, but nothing has taught me about the heart of our heavenly Father like being a dad. I love my kids like crazy, but they can also drive me crazy. And when they do, I'm reminded of God's infinite patience with our incessant whining, occasional temper tantrums, and blatant disobedience. Astounding, isn't it?

You'll lose your patience. You'll lose your temper. You might even lose your mind a time or two. You will make a million mistakes as a parent, but now for the good news: *your worst mistakes double as your greatest opportunities.*

How will your kids learn to apologize unless you model it for them by apologizing to them? Your mistakes give you the opportunity to model one of the most important lessons they'll ever learn—how to say "I'm sorry."

I have a very simple parenting philosophy that boils down to just three words: *please, sorry,* and *thanks.* If all else fails, I want to teach my kids to be really good at saying those three words—and then doing them! If they master *please*, *sorry*, and *thanks*, they are well on their way to a great marriages, great friendships, and a great relationship with God.

Finally, here's the great news: *prayer covers a multitude of sins.*

You'll never be a perfect parent, but you can be a praying parent. Prayer is your highest privilege as a parent. Don't just leverage it as a last resort when all else fails. Make it your first priority. Nothing you can do will give you a higher return on your investment, and the dividends are both generational and eternal. God will answer your prayers for your children long after you are gone. Prayer turns ordinary parents into prophets who shape the destinies of their children, grandchildren, and every generation that follows.

Prayer Genealogy

The blood running through my veins is 50 percent Swedish. I trace my genealogy back through the Johansson family, who made a decision to get on a boat and come to America in the late nineteenth century. That single decision set off a chain reaction that radically altered the destiny of every descendant to follow. That one decision made its mark on children, grandchildren, and great-grandchildren in more ways than I can possibly imagine.

Just as one decision can change your destiny, so can one prayer. If you were to map out your spiritual history, you would find countless answers to prayer at key intersections along the way. Before many of you were even born, even named, you had parents and grandparents who prayed for you. At critical ages and stages, family and friends interceded on your behalf. And thousands of complete strangers have prayed for you in ways you aren't even aware of. The sum total of those prayers is your prayer genealogy.

It's like your tree of life, your tree of Adam.

I believe that every blessing, every breakthrough, every miracle in your life traces back to the prayers that were prayed by you or for you. One of the greatest moments in eternity will be the day God peels back the space-time curtain and unveils His sovereignty by connecting the divine dots between our prayers and His answers. That infinite web of prayer crisscrosses every nation, every generation. And when God finally reveals His strange and mysterious ways, it will drop us to our knees in worship. We will thank Him for the prayers He *did* answer. We'll also thank Him for the prayers He *didn't* answer because we'll finally understand why. And we'll thank Him for the answered prayers we weren't even aware of.

My grandfather Elmer Johnson died when I was just six years old, but his prayers did not. Our prayers never die. They live on in the lives of those we pray for. Some of the most poignant and providential moments in my life have been the moments when the Spirit of God has whispered to my spirit, *Mark, the prayers of your grandfather are being answered in your life right now!*

My Grandpa Johnson had a habit of kneeling by his bed at night, taking off his hearing aid, and praying for his family. He couldn't hear himself, but everyone else in the house could. Few things are more powerful than hearing someone intercede on your behalf. His voiceprint left an imprint on my soul.

I'm trying to follow in my grandfather's footsteps by getting on my knees and praying next to my bed. It's a great way to start the day. My first thoughts and words are directed toward God. I also pray for my sleeping beauty lying a few feet away.

I realize that not everyone inherited a prayer legacy from their parents or grandparents as I did, but you can leave a legacy for future generations. You can start a new tradition, a new tree. You can begin a new prayer genealogy.

The Most Important Ten Minutes of the Day

The most important ten minutes of my day are the ten minutes I spend with my kids right before they leave for school. For many years, I felt like a failure when it came to leading my family in devotions. I could never seem to find a rhythm or a routine. It felt like one failed attempt after another. Then, the week before Parker started high school, Lora and I were on our Monday morning coffee date. Since I preach on Sundays, Monday is our Sabbath. We talk about our marriage, our kids, our calendar, and our finances. During the course of this particular conversation, I confessed my feeling of failure—and that's when Lora shared something her dad did, which I decided to adopt.

My father-in-law prayed with more intensity and more consistency than anybody I've ever known. That's why I dedicated *The Circle Maker* to Bob Schmidgall. He prayed about everything. In fact, when I asked him if I could marry his daughter, he literally said, "Let me pray about it." That'll put the fear of God in you—especially when he forgot to check back in for a week. Longest week of my life!

Bob Schmidgall was extraordinarily busy pastoring the church he founded in Naperville, Illinois, but he found time to do devotions with his four children every day before school. In the spirit of full disclosure, the teenage Lora didn't always enjoy those devotions. Most teenagers don't. But more than a decade after her dad's death, those devotional times they spent together are treasured memories. They were a daily touchpoint with her dad.

One of the great challenges with family devotions is finding a consistent time and place to pray together. It's not easy when your kids are playing soccer, taking piano lessons, participating in a school club, and taking swim lessons. And that's probably just one of your children! So how do you find a rhythm? I think it starts with looking at your daily routines. It makes sense to pray with your young children before bed because you tuck them in every night. With older children, it's more difficult because they probably will be staying up later than you do.

When Lora shared the story about morning devotions with her dad, it was a revelation. I knew I needed to leverage the first few minutes of the day before the day got away from me. So, beginning on Parker's first day of high school, I started reading the Bible and praying with him. Does every devotional time seem like a success? Hardly! Are there days when we're running late and have to scoot out of the house? Absolutely. But I'm determined to pray with my children, and that touchpoint is the most important ten minutes of my day. It's the most important meeting of the day. Why? Because I love my children so much more than anybody I'll meet with the rest of the day. And while every devotional time doesn't result in an epiphany, some of those touchpoints have turned into turning points.

Long After You Die

I know it's hard to find a consistent time and place to pray, but where there's a will, there's a way. And when it's God's will, He will help make a way.

Susanna Wesley gave birth to nineteen children, including John and Charles, the founders of the Methodist movement. There is no finding a quiet place to pray when you live in a small house with that many kids, but this reality didn't keep Susanna from praying. She would sit in her rocking chair in the middle of the living room, put a blanket over herself, and intercede for her children.[2]

Our excuses just went away, didn't they? Your children need to see and hear you praying. It doesn't matter whether it's in a prayer closet or a prayer chair. You can turn your commute or your workout into prayer times. When you make their beds or fold their clothes, pray for your kids. Go into their bedrooms while they're sleeping, kneel next to their beds, and pray over them.

You don't become a praying parent by default. You do it by design, by desire, by discipline. Spiritual disciplines take sheer determination, but if you determine to circle your children in prayer, your prayers will shape their destinies, just as Susanna Wesley's prayers shaped the destinies of her children. Your prayers will live on in their lives long after you die.

Your prayers for your children are the greatest legacy you can leave.

Chapter 2

The Legend
of the Circle Maker

*"Truly, I say to you, whatever you bind on earth
shall be bound in heaven, and whatever you
loose on earth shall be loosed in heaven. Again
I say to you, if two of you agree on earth about
anything they ask, it will be done for them by
my Father in heaven. For where two or three are
gathered in my name, there am I among them."*

MATTHEW 18:18–20 ESV

first discovered the legend of Honi the Circle Maker while reading *The Book of Legends*, a compilation of stories from the Hebrew Talmud and Midrash. And that legend has radically changed the way I pray. It gave me a new vocabulary and a new methodology. For those who haven't read *The Circle Maker,* let me share the legend behind the book. But instead of the adult version, let me share the storyline from the bedtime picture book *The Circle Maker for Kids.* If you have young children, you might want to pick up the illustrated version and read it to them before bed.

It had not rained in Israel for one entire year.
No clouds in the sky. No water in the well.
Gardens did not grow. Rivers ran dry.
Dust filled the air.

The people were thirsty and scared. They pleaded with one voice, "O God, give us rain!" But when God didn't answer right away, they lost faith. Some feared He had forgotten them. Then they remembered something, remembered someone.

The rainmaker.

Hardly anyone had seen his face, but nearly everyone had heard his voice. People would travel for days just to hear Honi praying inside his hut on the outskirts of Jerusalem. Like Elijah, who ended a three-year drought with one prayer, Honi was famous for praying for rain. He had the same faith, the same spirit. The people knew that Honi was their last hope, their only hope. So they knocked, and the rainmaker answered. He boldly declared, "The same God who made thunder will make it clap. The same God who made the clouds will make them rain."

A parade of people led Honi into the city, to the Temple Mount. As the crowd grew larger, children climbed onto the shoulders of their fathers. Others stood on tiptoe to see what Honi would say, what Honi would do. And that's when it happened.

Honi bowed his head and extended his staff to the ground. Then he began to turn. He turned all the way around until he stood inside the complete circle he had drawn. Then, with the hope of the entire nation on his shoulders, Honi dropped to his knees. A holy hush came over the crowd so that everyone heard his humble prayer.

"Sovereign Lord, I swear before Your Great Name that I will not leave this circle until You have mercy upon Your children."

Like water from a well, the words flowed from the depths of his soul. The people watched and waited. Then it happened. A single raindrop fell from the sky.

"That is not enough water!" the people grumbled. Still kneeling within the circle, Honi continued to pray to God with a humble heart. "Not for such rain have I prayed, but for rain that will fill cisterns, pits, and caverns."

Lightning flashed.

Thunder clapped.

The sprinkle turned into such a downpour that the crowd fled to higher ground to escape the flash floods. Not Honi. He battled the storm on his knees. "Not for such rain have I prayed, but for rain of Your favor, blessing, and graciousness."

Then, like a cool shower on a hot summer day, it began to rain calmly, peacefully. Parents opened their mouths to catch the falling raindrops. Children danced in the downpour like it was the first rainfall they had ever seen. Laughter filled the air.

It was the day thunderclaps applauded God.

It was the day puddle jumping became an act of praise.

It was the day the true legend of the Circle Maker was born.

The rainmaker would forever be known as Honi the Circle Maker. The Circle Maker had taught them the power of prayer. They now knew that one prayer can change anything. One prayer can change everything. And from that day forth, whenever the people needed a miracle, they would draw a circle and pray just like Honi. They circled the sick. They circled the sad. They circled the young. They circled the old. They circled their biggest dreams. They circled their *greatest fears. And, most importantly, they circled the promises of God.*

Sometimes they had to pray for a long, long time. But they never again doubted the fact that God always hears. And if our prayers glorify God, God always answers. Everyone who witnessed the miracle that day learned a lesson they would never forget: God honors bold prayers because bold prayers honor God.

The Prayer That Saved a Generation

Now here's the rest of the story.

Some members of the Sanhedrin wanted to excommunicate Honi because they believed his prayer was too bold, but it's awfully hard to argue with a miracle! Ultimately, Honi was honored for "the prayer that saved a generation."

I love that commendation: *the prayer that saved a generation.*

An entire generation of Jews traced their

genealogy back to one man, one prayer. Just like Honi, your prayers have the power to save the next generation. You can't choose Christ for your kids, but you can pray that they choose Christ. And I've met far too many children who have come to Christ because their parents prevailed in prayer, sometimes for decades, to believe God for anything less. What other option do we have? To pray or not to pray—these are the only options.

Let me offer one word of advice to parents of prodigals: form a prayer circle with other parents. Covenant to pray for each other's children. Why other parents? Because no one can pray for children the way parents can! We all have similar hopes, similar heartbreaks. Other parents love their children just like you love yours. And empathy is high-octane fuel for intercession.

Lora and I were having dinner with friends recently when they revealed that their nineteen-year-old daughter, whom we've known since she was a little girl, had walked away from God and started living with her boyfriend. God gave us a supernatural burden for our friend's daughter, and we started fighting for her in prayer. In the months that followed, a spiritual shift took place. We discovered that she not only started attending church again, but she started attending the church we pastor! Her next move was moving out of her boyfriend's apartment. She has since recommitted her life to Christ and begun a gap year serving God with a mission organization.

Lora and I obviously don't take credit for everything God has done in this young woman's life, but we did take responsibility when we found out she needed intercessory prayer. And I'm grateful for the people in my prayer circle who intercede for my children on a daily basis. Parenting is a tag-team sport. Sometimes you need to tap out and let a spouse or prayer partner tap in. We need to stand in the gap for one another's children—or maybe I should say *kneel* in the gap. Teens also need a few non-parental voices that will speak into their lives. There will be stages and ages where your children might listen to other adults even though they aren't listening to you.

Also, realize that your prayers function as prophecies. You script the future of your family with your prayers just as my grandfather did for me. Am I stretching the truth? Not at all. I'm simply circling the promise in Psalm 103:17 (NKJV):

> But the mercy of the LORD is from everlasting
> to everlasting
> On those who fear Him,
> And His righteousness to children's children.

Jesus Christ broke the curse of sin at Calvary and secured for us every spiritual blessing as our inheritance (Ephesians 1:3). This is our birthright as children of our heavenly Father, and it is our responsibility as parents to pass down this generational blessing to our earthly children.

But maybe you were the victim of abuse, you didn't have a father, or you were the child of a divorce. Maybe you never felt loved or always felt shamed by your parents when you were growing up. And now you're afraid you'll make the same mistakes. You need to know that Jesus Christ broke the curse so you can break the cycle! This doesn't mean it'll happen quickly or easily. But if you *pray through*, you'll eventually experience the breakthrough. You won't just be blessed; you'll pass on a blessing to the next generation.

Drawing Circles

Since the release of *The Circle Maker*, I've had a steady stream of e-mails and letters from readers who have started circling their dreams, their homes, and their workplaces in prayer. An inner-city teacher circles her classroom every morning, and a real estate agent circles the properties she represents as listing agent. A team of doctors and nurses circles their patients as they make hospital rounds. Several members of Congress are circling the Capitol, and a member of the president's travel pool is circling the White House. And at least one NFL head coach is circling his team's stadium before every home game. One of my favorite testimonies was from the reader who started circling his bank praying for a financial miracle—until law enforcement intervened because they thought he was casing it.

There is nothing magical about physically circling something in prayer, but there is something biblical about it. The Israelites circled the city of Jericho until the wall came down (Joshua 5:13–6:21). What if they had quit circling after six laps? Or what if they had given up on the sixth day? They would have forfeited the miracle right before it happened. We tend to give up too quickly, too easily. We need to circle our Jericho until the wall comes tumbling down.

You can circle anything in prayer, but nothing is more important to circle than your children. Does that mean you circle them like you're playing a game of Duck Duck Goose? Not unless you want to get dizzy! Drawing prayer circles is a metaphor that means *to pray without ceasing*. It's asking until God answers. It's praying with more intensity, more tenacity. It's not just *praying for*; it's *praying through*. There are times when you have to grab on to the horns of the altar and pray until your knees are numb. We instinctively attach an *ASAP* to every prayer and ask God to answer *as soon as possible.* We need a paradigm shift. We need to start praying *ALAIT* prayers—*as long as it takes.* That's what praying circles is all about. It's resolving in your heart of hearts that you will keep praying until the day you die.

84,315 Prayers

I love the story my friend Wayne told me about his grandmother who did just that: she prayed until the day she died. Raising a dozen children while managing household duties was no easy task, but that didn't keep her from praying. After every meal, Wayne's grandmother would lock herself in her bedroom to pray. Three times a day, the children could hear her interceding for them by name.

When Grandma Cook was on her deathbed at the age of ninety-one, the entire family gathered at the family home. She invited them into the bedroom where she had prayed three times a day every day. Then she prophetically declared to her twelve children, "I'm going to die, but the power of my prayers will come to pass in each of your lives."

Her predominant prayer was that every member of her family would surrender their lives to the lordship of Jesus Christ. At the time, six children were following Christ and six weren't. That was fifteen years ago. The tally is now ten *yes* and two *no*—or maybe I should say, in faith, *two not yet*. Wayne shared with me how the tenth child, the oldest child, said yes to Christ.

> My grandmother's oldest son is named Johnny. A month ago, his next-door neighbor had a dream in the middle of the night about Johnny. The neighbor felt compelled to invite him to church, and he accepted the invitation that Sunday, which happened to be Palm Sunday. When he walked into that church, all he could hear was his mother's voice calling out his name in prayer. The pastor asked if anybody wanted to put their

faith in Jesus, and Johnny raised his ninety-two-year-old hand. He got baptized the next weekend on Easter Sunday.

I did the math. Wayne's grandmother passed away when Johnny was seventy-seven years old. From the day he was born until the day she died, she prayed for him three times a day. If you add it up, that is 84,315 prayers! She didn't get to see the answer to her prayers on the temporal side of the space-time continuum, but she will be the first one to greet her son when he steps into eternity!

Did her prayers have anything to do with the neighbor's middle-of-the-night dream? I cannot imagine that they did not. And that is the beauty of prayer. We never know when or how our prayers will be answered. And we never know when we—just like Johnny's neighbor—will be the answer to someone else's prayer. You might be the answer to 84,315 prayers! But when you live by faith, you can be confident that you will harvest prayer seeds that have been planted for years, for decades, even for centuries. When you live by faith, the prayer offerings you made while your children lived under your roof will one day turn into praise offerings that will raise the roof in heaven.

Secret Weapon

I'm a connoisseur of testimonies. And the most poignant prayer testimonies I've received over the years come from parents who are circling their children in prayer like never before. Parents are praying the promises of God around their children. They are interceding for future spouses, believing for miracles, and praying a hedge of protection around their children. And parents aren't just praying that God would keep their kids safe; they're also praying that He will make them dangerous for His purposes so they can make a difference in their generation. That is the kind of prayer God loves to answer. May God raise up a generation of circle makers who will pray hard, pray bold, and pray through!

One of the most moving testimonies I know of comes from my friend Craig Johnson. Craig and his wife, Samantha, have three children. Their youngest son, Connor, has autism. Like many parents of kids with special needs, Craig and Samantha found themselves teeter-tottering between hope and despair, faith and discouragement. Then they got a copy of *The Circle Maker* and decided it was time to start circling, start believing, start praying again.

Can I come right out and say it? Parenting is the hardest thing you'll ever do. And the more you love your kids, the harder it is. It is spiritually, emotionally, and relationally taxing. And this challenge is multiplied for parents of children with special needs. It takes a heroic effort, and this is exactly what the parents of special needs kids are in my book: heroes. The parenting they do takes a special anointing.

Craig and Samantha read about the importance of *praying the Word*, so they decided to circle thirty biblical promises and begin to pray them around Connor. What they didn't know is that Connor was memorizing them—all of them. Without even knowing it, they were planting seeds of faith in his heart. They started by praying these promises before he went to sleep at night, and then Connor asked them to pray the promises in the morning too.

Because of his autism, Connor struggles with controlling his emotions, so he sometimes experiences dramatic meltdowns and mood changes. But Connor is now reciting Scripture as a way of helping himself cope. One day, Craig wouldn't let Connor play with their iPad, and Connor quoted from Psalms: "Lord, save me from the pit" (Psalm 69:15 TLB). Craig and Samantha laughed at first, but then they cried as they realized that their son was hiding the Word of God in his heart. Another day, Connor cut his foot, and while Samantha put hydrogen peroxide on it, he cried out from James: "Is anyone among you sick? Let him call for the elders of the church, and let them pray over him" (James 5:14 ESV). Samantha stared in disbelief.

One of the many challenges Craig and Samantha faced was the simple fact that, at eight years of age, Connor wasn't potty trained. So they decided to circle Connor and pray for a miracle. I'll never forget what Craig said: "Mark, what one person may see as ordinary, another may see as his miracle."

Then Craig told me that not long after they started circling Connor and believing for this miracle, Connor came in from playing outside and, for the first time in his life, went to the bathroom all by himself. Craig started crying as he told me the story; then I started crying. Craig said, "After what seemed like years of drought, God began to send the abundance of rain."

Connor stopped having severe meltdowns. He started eating vegetables and losing some excess weight. Instead of simply repeating everything that was spoken to him, Connor started to respond. And he even tied his own shoelaces for the very first time! Does this mean the final battle has been fought? We know better; we're parents! The challenges never end, but we need to celebrate the victories along the way. And for the record, prayer is the way we parents best fight our battles. Prayer is the difference between *you fighting for God* and *God fighting for you.*

Secret prayer is our secret weapon.

When we get on our knees, God extends His powerful right hand on our behalf.

For the record, Craig and Samantha aren't just circling their own children. They are promoting a cause by starting Champions Clubs and Champions Academies (development centers and charter schools) that will serve children with special needs all across the country.[3]

The earth has circled the sun more than two thousand times since the day Honi drew his circle in the sand, but God is still looking for circle makers. He is still looking for those who dream big and pray hard. And drawing prayer circles starts with the family circle!

Chapter 3

Seven Prayer Circles

Rise during the night and cry out.
    Pour out your hearts like water to the
        Lord.
Lift up your hands to him in prayer,
    pleading for your children.

LAMENTATIONS 2:19 NLT

L et me formally introduce you to my wife and our three children.

Lora and I are high school sweethearts. We dated all the way through college and got married two weeks after graduation. We have been happily married for twenty years, and we'll celebrate our twenty-second anniversary next year. Yes, you read that right. The first two years were rough sailing. We were both very young and very stubborn, but we weathered the storm, and those tough times have helped us appreciate the good times.

Lora and I decided to start our family young. It felt like we were kids when we had our kids. We were high on energy and low on wisdom. Seventeen years and three children later, we have a little more wisdom and a lot less energy!

Our oldest son, Parker, is now eighteen.

Summer Joy is sixteen going on twenty-one.

And Josiah is eleven.

I honestly thought we'd have more children when we got married. I wanted five kids so we could field a complete basketball team, but a near-death experience that required several surgeries to repair ruptured intestines interrupted our family planning. So three it was, and three it is. I like to describe it this way: our energy is divided by three, but our joy is multiplied by three.

Let me come right out and say it: I don't love my kids equally. No parent does. I love them uniquely. Their passions and personalities couldn't be more different, which means we had to learn how to parent all over again with each of them. They respond to discipline very differently, and they speak different love languages. Taking my daughter shopping is one way I express my love for her, but my boys would see it as form of discipline!

I have come to terms with the fact that I've done more things wrong than I've done right as a parent, but I've taken courage from the simple fact that it's not just my wife and I who are raising our kids. We have a heavenly Father who compensates for our deficiencies, weaknesses, and mistakes! We don't only have our children double-teamed. They're actually triple-teamed by the Father, Son, and Holy Spirit. The Father is their heavenly Father. The Son is their Advocate against the adversary. And the Holy Spirit is interceding for them around the clock with groanings that cannot be uttered in words (Romans 8:26). So where we fail as earthly parents, I believe the Father, Son, and Holy Spirit can succeed.

Parent or Prophet?

If you asked me what I pray for as a parent more than anything else, the answer is the favor of God. While it's difficult to describe or define, *the favor of God is what God can do for you that you cannot do for yourself.*

When Parker was a baby, I circled Luke 2:52 and turned it into a prayer blessing. I have prayed this blessing around each of my children thousands of times. Almost every night when they were young, I tucked them into bed with this simple prayer: *Lord, let them grow in wisdom and stature and in favor with God and with man.*

I realize that Luke 2:52 isn't technically a promise, but I think I'm on sound theological ground. This one verse is a time-lapse of Jesus' development as a child, and we're called to be just like Jesus, so why wouldn't I circle it? Why shouldn't I turn it into a blessing and pray it around my children?

Please listen to me, parents: *you are a prophet to your children.*

Jewish philosophers did not believe the prophetic gift was reserved for a few select individuals. They believed that becoming prophetic was the crowning point of mental and spiritual development. It was the natural by-product of spiritual development. The more one grows in grace, the more prophetic one becomes. This doesn't mean you will start predicting the future; it actually means you'll start creating it. How? Through your prayers!

Prayer is the way we write the future. It's the difference between *letting things happen* and *making things happen*.

Personal Prophecies

I once read that at least 40 percent of our lives are based on personal prophecies.[4] I'm not sure how you substantiate a statistic like that, but I find it very believable. The right word spoken at the right time can make an eternal difference.

We all need personal prophets in our lives. And I pray that my children encounter a lot of people who have a profoundly positive influence on their lives. Right at the top of the list are some of the unsung heroes of the kingdom—youth pastors. I'm deeply grateful for youth pastors who tag-team with me as a parent, but let me make one thing clear: it's not their responsibility to disciple my children. That's *my* responsibility! You cannot delegate discipleship any more than you can delegate prayer.

You need to speak words of comfort and encouragement to your children (1 Corinthians 14:3). When you catch them doing something wrong, gently rebuke them. Lovingly remind them, "That's not who you are." They are acting out of character, the character of Christ. And when you catch your children doing something right, reinforce it. Fan into flame the gift of God that is in them.

In the pages that follow, I want to share seven biblical and practical ways to circle your kids in prayer. But before we start circling, let me offer a few guidelines. First, you don't have to do all seven simultaneously. In fact, I encourage you to focus on one or two of them at a time. Second, you won't master these approaches to prayer right away. Prayer takes practice, and practice makes perfect. But if you stick with it, these prayer habits will become second nature. Finally, ask the Holy Spirit to give you your own ideas. Don't just *adopt* these habits; *adapt* them to your unique situation, your unique personality, and your children's unique personalities.

Let's draw the first circle.

Chapter 4

The 1st Circle:
Circling the Promises of God

No matter how many promises God
has made, they are "Yes" in Christ.

2 Corinthians 1:20

One of my most memorable moments as a parent happened during Parker's kindergarten graduation ceremony. One by one, each child in his class shared his or her life dream while parents waited with bated breath. Many of them had noble aspirations, but none compared to that of my son. I'll never forget the words that came out of his six-year-old mouth: "I want the whole world to know Jesus." I almost burst into tears! I could have died and gone to parent heaven. I felt like we had reached the zenith of parenthood, and it had only taken six years to get there. All of our hopes for Parker were encapsulated in that one statement—but it was short-lived.

After the ceremony I asked Parker about his dream, hoping that perhaps he had been inspired by his father. That's when he dropped the bummer bomb by telling us that his teachers had told him what to say! And it got worse. Parker said, "That's not really my dream. I want to be a construction man." Now listen, there is nothing wrong with the construction profession, but that seems like a half step down from telling the whole world about Jesus!

I experienced a degree of disappointment at first, but the more I thought about it, the more I loved how honest Parker's answer was. He wasn't trying to be who I wanted him to be, and that's both healthy and holy. Few things are more difficult or more necessary than individuation. All parents have dreams for their children, and if you aren't careful, you'll psychologically project your unfulfilled dreams onto your children instead of letting them blaze their own trails. Your children are not you. They have a unique destiny to fulfill, and you get to play a key part. But make sure you're praying, not projecting! There is a fine line between your will and God's will. Make sure you are praying His will for your children, not yours.

Every prayer, including your prayers for your children, must pass this twofold litmus test: they must be in the will of God and for the glory of God. God is not a genie in a bottle, and your wish is not His command. Actually, His command better be your wish. If it's not, you won't be drawing prayer circles; you'll just end up walking in circles. Drawing prayer circles starts with discerning what God wants, what God wills. And the best place to start is the promises of God.

Prophet-Historian

One of our primary responsibilities as parents is helping our children discover the unique role they play in God's redemptive story. In order to do so, we have to become students of our children. Your children are the most important *subject* you'll ever study! And far more complicated than calculus!

Parents are not only prophets who speak into their children's future, but we are also historians who record their past. In one sense, you know your children better than they know themselves. They can't remember their first few years of life, but you cannot forget them. You remember their first words, their first steps, and their first day of school as if it were yesterday.

You have a unique vantage point as a parent. No one sees the past, present, and future quite like you do. It's your job to help your children connect the dots between who they *were*, who they *are*, and who they *are becoming*. One of the ways I've done that is by writing an annual letter to my children capturing moments I don't want us to forget. I was a better journalist when our kids were younger, but here's the latest letter I wrote to Summer on her sixteenth birthday.

My Sweet Sixteen,

You were up to my knees yesterday.

Today you turn sixteen.

Where did 5840 days go?

Part of me wants to slow down time, but I love who you're becoming too much to do that. And no matter how old you get, you will always be my little girl. You have become more beautiful than I could have ever imagined. You have brought more joy to my life than you will ever know. I thought my life was complete before you were born, but I was wrong. Something was missing and it was you—my one and only daughter.

When I look at you, my heart swells. You are my pride and joy. I'm so grateful that God chose me to be your dad.

If all the girls in the world were lined up and I could only choose one . . . I'd choose you.

Sixteen kisses,

Dad

I'm honestly not sure how significant that letter was to Summer on the day I gave it to her, but like an antique, it will gain value with the passage of time. If she keeps it long enough, it might become a keepsake—a token of her father's love for her.

Soulprint

As students of our children, we are to help them discover the God-ordained passions and God-given gifts that make them unique. There never has been and never will be anyone like them, and that fact isn't a testament to our children. It's a testament to the God who created them. Our uniqueness is God's gift to us, but it's also our gift back to God. So while we owe it to ourselves to be ourselves, more importantly, we owe it to God. We don't need to be more like Billy Graham or Mother Teresa; each one of us needs to be more like the person God created us to be. After all, if you is who you ain't, then you ain't who you is.

One challenge our children face is that peer pressure has a way of beating the individuality out of them. The way we combat cultural conformity is via unconditional love and unrelenting prayer. Our attempts to bolster our children's self-esteem are misguided if those attempts are self-centered. Self-esteem comes from placing supreme value on God, not self. Anything less is idolatry. Our value comes from this simple yet profound truth: *no one else can worship God like you or for you.* That's what makes each one of us invaluable and irreplaceable.

Just like our unique fingerprint and voiceprint,

we have a soulprint. And I define *soulprint* as our unique identity and destiny in Christ that differentiates us from everyone else on the planet. It's our job as parents to help our children discover their soulprint, and that may be the most important discovery they'll ever make.

I want my children to be comfortable in their own skin, but that requires far more than skin-deep self-awareness. They have to dig deep into their souls and discover what lies beneath the surface. Writer Fredrick Buechner describes the process of self-discovery this way:

> Beneath the face I am a family plot. All the people I have ever been are buried there—the bouncing boy, his mother's pride; the pimply boy and secret sensualist; the reluctant infantryman; the beholder at dawn through hospital plate-glass of his first-born child. All these selves I was I am no longer, not even the bodies they wore are my body any longer, and although when I try, I can remember scraps and pieces about them, I can

no longer remember what it felt like to live inside their skin. Yet they live inside my skin to this day, they are buried in me somewhere, ghosts that certain songs, tastes, smells, sights, tricks of weather can raise, and although I am not the same as they, I am not different either because their having been them is responsible for my being now.[5]

Buechner then adds this caveat: "Buried in me too are all the people I have not been yet but might be someday."[6] That is certainly true of our children. And it's our job to help them discover that God-ordained destiny.

Your True Name

Some of the hardest decisions Lora and I have ever made were what to name our children. No easy task. But let me take a little pressure off you if you're pregnant. No matter what you decide to name your children, it's not their real name. The name you give them is really just a pseudonym. Revelation 2:17 reveals that God will one day give us a white stone with a new name written on it, a name unknown to anyone besides our Creator. It's a name He gave us before we were born, and it will only be revealed after we die. And when God finally reveals our true name, it will unveil our true identity. Until then, we have to rely on the nickname given to us by our earthly parents. We also have to rely on our earthly parents to help us discover who we are. Let me explain.

Half of your role as prophet-historian is to *know your children*. The other half is to *know Scripture*. They are like the parallel rails of a train track that, together, enable us to train our children in the way they should go (Proverbs 22:6).

When our children enter a new season of life, it is full of uncertainty and insecurity. Kids can experience an identity crisis because they aren't sure where they fit or who they are. When they enter middle school or high school or college, we need to intercede for our children. At these critical intersections, we need to pray that our sons and daughters will make the right friends and the right choices . . . that their conscience will keep them from taking the path of least resistance . . . and that they won't just survive tough situations, but grow stronger because of them.

If your kids have a difficult time discerning or doing the will of God, you may have to agonize in prayer for them the way Jesus did in Gethsemane. This kind of prayer is part of parenthood. You have to pray the price—and the price is blood, sweat, and tears.

Holy Confidence

I spent several agonizing hours interceding for Summer recently as she made what I felt was a critical decision. She had decided to try out for the freshman volleyball team even though she had never played organized volleyball before. I felt added responsibility because she did so with my strong encouragement.

On the first day of tryouts, all four grades played together, and she felt overwhelmed by the talent level of some of the seniors who were NCAA Division 1 caliber players. Summer decided to quit after the first day, but I felt like she should stick with it. I didn't want her first experience with high school to be dropping out of a tryout, but I also empathized with her. To make matters worse, I wasn't home because I was hiking Half Dome in Yosemite National Park with Parker. For the record, these kinds of situations always seem to happen when I'm out of town!

I was on the phone with Summer and Lora for several hours that night. I didn't know what to do or what to say, but I knew we needed to pray. Our hike was scheduled to start before sunrise the next morning, but I couldn't sleep that night. I spent several hours in the shadow of Half Dome praying that God would give Summer the courage she needed to keep going. I also prayed that something would happen to change her mind, but I had no idea what that something might be.

The next day the varsity volleyball coach called our house. Are you kidding me? He didn't have to do that. I honestly couldn't believe it. Well, that phone call was the catalyst that got Summer to go back and try out. I was so proud of her! And I wasn't proud just because she made the team and had a great season; I was proud because she swallowed her pride, faced her fears, and took a risk.

I know this situation may not sound significant to you, and it certainly wasn't a matter of life or death, but I just felt in my spirit that returning to the tryouts would set an important precedent in Summer's life. This was the kind of thing that could either give her confidence or rob her of confidence.

Since that night of intercession, one of my recurrent prayers for Summer is that she will grow in confidence. I'm not talking about self-confidence. I'm praying for the *holy confidence* that comes from doing the will of God for the glory of God. It's a confidence that is anchored in the power of God, the grace of God, and the word of God. So over the next several months, I searched for any and every verse of Scripture that spoke of confidence, and I read those passages to Summer before school during our ten-minute devotional time. I wanted those promises to get into her spirit, into her subconscious.

The Peace That Transcends Understanding

Josiah is at a very different age and stage. Most of our prayers revolve around his fears. These fears can be frustrating at times, but patience is the by-product of remembering some of our own childhood challenges.

For me, the big one was Bigfoot. I was convinced he lived under my bed or in my closet, and my brother didn't help matters. Our family tradition was saying good night from our respective rooms, so I would yell into the darkness, "Good night, Mom. Good night, Dad. Good night, Don." My brother would respond, "Good night, Mom. Good night, Dad. Good night,

Mark. Good night, Bigfoot." Got me every time! My mom and dad would have to get up and redo the closet check and bed check.

Now here's the thing: my fear was totally irrational. If Bigfoot could fit in my closet or under my bed, he wasn't really that big! But you cannot reason with irrational fears. *Irrational fears submit only to prayer.*

And our most powerful prayers are hyperlinked to the promises of God. One of my favorites is found in Philippians 4:6–7:

> Do not be anxious about anything, but in every situation, by prayer and petition, with thanksgiving, present your requests to God. And the peace of God, which transcends all understanding, will guard your hearts and your minds in Christ Jesus.

I'm praying this promise, and Josiah is memorizing it. He is learning that when we circle the promises of God, those promises then encircle us.

The peace that transcends understanding literally guards our hearts and minds.

Love God and Love Girls

One of the promises that God put into my heart to pray for Parker is that he will grow up to *love God* and *love girls*. The first one is obvious: I'm praying that Parker will be great at obeying the Great Commandment. I'm praying that he'll love God with all his heart and soul and mind and strength. That's true greatness.

Let me explain the second part: *love girls*.

I'm praying that Parker understands and appreciates the created order: "male and female [God] created them" (Genesis 1:27). I'm praying that Parker will honor the opposite sex, starting with the women who are already in his life—his mother and his sister. And I'm praying that Parker ultimately meets and marries a girl he can grow old with, a girl he can grow in God with.

We live in a culture full of sexual brokenness, and I think it's the by-product of sexual confusion. Part of the problem is that churches are answering questions that no one is asking instead of talking about what everybody is thinking about. Sex is at the top of the list, and the Bible is explicit in its teaching about it. Sex is a sacred covenant between a husband and a wife to be enjoyed in the context of a marriage covenant. Of course, our culture begs to differ. In fact, our culture tells us it's wrong to say something is wrong, and I think that's wrong. If we don't use our voice, we lose our voice.

One of our sacred responsibilities is to teach our kids the difference between right and wrong, and nowhere is this more necessary than in our approach to the topic of sexuality. We need to celebrate sex as a gift from God: sex is not just a good thing; it's a God thing. We also need to help our children understand that sex is a playground, but it has a fence around it called marriage. Sex outside the marriage covenant is sin—and I'm not just talking about adultery. Biblically speaking, sex before marriage is cheating on your future spouse. Of course, we have to be as graceful as we are truthful. After all, it's tough for our kids to be truthful if we aren't graceful.

Now here's my advice when it comes to teaching our kids about sexuality: *don't just say it; pray it.* You certainly have to have "the talk," but you also need to circle Psalm 37:4:

> *Take delight in the LORD,*
> *and he will give you the desires of your*
> *heart.*

This promise isn't a blank check. It doesn't mean that God will give you whatever you want. Quite the contrary! It means that if you genuinely delight yourself in the Lord, then the Spirit of God will radically change your desires. There is no doubt that old desires die hard. In fact, they seem to have nine lives, and sexual desires are some of the hardest desires to change. But dying to self means dying to our sinful desires. And the Holy Spirit promises to conceive within you new desires, holy desires.

So don't just pray that your teenager doesn't

get pregnant; pray that your son or daughter gets pregnant with the Holy Spirit. Don't just pray defensively that your children won't do anything wrong; pray that they'll do something right. Don't just pray that God keeps them safe and sound; pray that He'd makes them dangerous for His purposes.

Pray the Promises

If you are feeling overwhelmed or you don't know where to begin, pray the promises of God. It's almost like downloading updates to your operating system. You are simultaneously upgrading your conscience so it is fine-tuned to the Holy Spirit and Holy Scripture. And that's what enables you as a parent to let go and let God—when you are confident that your children will let their conscience be their guide.

As I said earlier, our most powerful prayers are hyperlinked to the promises of God. When we know we are praying the promises of God, we can pray with holy confidence. We don't have to second-guess ourselves, because we know that God's Word does not return void (Isaiah 55:11). This doesn't mean we can claim the promises of God out of context or claim them for someone else. But our problem as believers isn't *over*claiming the promises of God; it's *under*claiming them. But if we stand on God's Word, God will stand by His Word.

I've prayed Luke 2:52 thousands of times for my children. And while I don't always notice the tangible evidence of God answering those prayers, I know that what goes around in prayer comes around. So I'm not surprised by the favor my kids have found at critical junctures in their lives. That's their destiny! They have to choose the straight-and-narrow path, but God is preparing good works in advance for them.

My son, Parker, recently co-led a mission trip to South Africa. During the trip, one of the team members sent me a short e-mail commenting on Parker's prophetic anointing: "Just wanted to let you know that some of your Luke 2:52 prayers are coming to fruition with Parker. Awesome being on this mission trip with him. Love that guy!"

As my children mature into adulthood, I fully expect them to experience ridiculous favor for which there is no earthly explanation. I've asked thousands of times; I expect thousands of answers!

Fallback Position

Let me offer a word of encouragement for those times when you face discouragement as a parent. When you are in the depths of parenting despair, when things look hopeless and you feel helpless, you need to keep circling the promises of God. I have a handful of Bible verses that I call fallback positions. When I am at my weakest, they are the promises I fall back on with my full faith. One of those particularly helpful fallback positions for parents is inspired by Isaiah 61:3:

> *[Put on] the garment of praise for the spirit of heaviness. (NKJV)*

Nothing can produce pure joy like our children, but they can also break our hearts by the things they say or do. Whether it's a toddler who discovers the word *no,* a teenager who rebels against everything you believe in, or an adult child who goes through a painful divorce, you will experience "the spirit of heaviness" that the prophet Isaiah referenced. And that's when I pray in the Spirit because I'm not sure what to pray on my own. I also put on "the garment of praise" because that's what Isaiah prescribed. Over time, the garment of praise will become like your favorite pair of jeans that fit like a glove. You will need to pull them out of your prayer closet often. And don't take off the garment of praise until the spirit of heaviness evaporates like morning fog.

Recently, I met a husband and wife who were heartbroken because of a broken relationship with their son. When their son told them he was gay, they didn't know how to respond. The son as well as the parents made some mistakes and said some things they later regretted. It had been a decade since they had last talked to him, and their spirit of heaviness was painfully obvious.

When this couple heard the legend of Honi the Circle Maker, they felt it was time to start circling again. We actually held hands and formed a prayer circle on the spot. Less than a month later, their prodigal son came home. Is there a lot of healing that must still take place? Absolutely. You don't solve ten years of problems in ten minutes or ten days. I'm not saying that God cannot bring immediate healing or instantaneous deliverance, but we often have to get out of problems the way we got into them—one step at a time. Prayer is the first step. And that one small step can turn into a giant leap.

Chapter 5

The 2nd Circle: Making Prayer Lists

Listen to my voice in the morning, LORD.
Each morning I bring my requests to you
and wait expectantly.

PSALM 5:3 NLT

'm the worst grocery shopper in the world. I rarely bring home everything I was supposed to get, and I always bring home something I shouldn't have gotten. Why? Probably because I don't shop with a grocery list. Evidently I'm not alone. Supermarket studies have found that while nearly 100 percent of women come armed with a shopping list, less than 25 percent of men carry a list. Between 60 and 70 percent of all grocery purchases made by men are unplanned. The study also revealed an area in which men outshop women—junk food.[7] Hail to the male gender!

I know that making lists isn't part of everybody's personality, and making lists doesn't sound very exciting, but is there a better way to make sure we do what needs to be done? And if we need a grocery list, an invite list, and a to-do list, is it possible we need a prayer list?

The goal of a prayer list is not to simply lay out a laundry list before God. In fact, prayer is not about our agenda for God at all; it's about discovering God's agenda for us. But once we discover His agenda, we have to write it down. In my experience, it's very difficult to pray with specificity, intentionality, and consistency without a prayer list. And for the record, I encourage you to keep a record. Then you can give God the glory when He answers your prayers.

John and Susan Yates have pastored The Falls Church just outside Washington, D.C., for more than three decades, and during that time they raised their five children. Before their daughter Alison was married, she told her dad that some of her earliest and most meaningful memories of childhood were hearing him in his study praying for their family before the crack of dawn. That comment inspired John to go back through his old journals and look at the long list of things he had prayed for over the years. Those prayers ranged from asking

God to give Alison a better appetite at mealtimes when she was four to praying that books would thrill her when she was seven. Like many parents, he prayed for her academic and athletic endeavors with great fervor during her middle years. And he prayed for an especially close relationship with his daughter, which his prayers helped forge. John also prayed for Alison's future husband, Will, for many years before they met or married. Those prayer lists have become one of John's most prized possessions because they are a record of God's faithfulness in Alison's life.

For what it's worth, Lora and I got a great idea from John and Susan that we've tucked away for when we're grandparents. Every summer they have a Cousins Camp at their farm in rural Virginia for all of their grandchildren over the age of four. Grandpa and Grandma serve as co-directors of the camp, and those camps have helped keep them a close-knit family despite the fact that their children have moved out and moved away from home.

Prayer Journal

At the beginning of the calendar year, Lora and I spent one of our coffee dates making a prayer list for our children. Some of these prayers are probably prayers that every parent prays for their children, but we also tried to personalize our list based on the unique personalities and passions of our children.

One of the prayers that made the list is this: "Lord, let their ears be tuned to the still, small voice of the Holy Spirit." I want my children to *find their voice*, and the key is *hearing the voice of God*. If they don't hear the voice of God, they will echo our culture. But if they listen to God, people will listen to them, and they'll become a voice to their generation. I want my children to have a prophetic voice, and that starts with having a prophetic ear. So I am specifically praying that God will give them the ear of Samuel (1 Samuel 3:1–10).

I can't wait to someday show my children the prayers I have journaled for them. Some of them I have already revealed, but some I won't share until those prayers are answered. One way or another, we need to document our prayers by writing them in a prayer journal. Journal like a journalist, because that's what you are to your children.

I have a friend whose father journaled prayers for her and her two sisters without them even knowing it. In fact, my friend didn't find out about the prayer journals until after her father died. Those journals are one of her most treasured possessions. Imagine being able to go back and see what your parents were praying for you two or twelve or twenty years ago. One thing is certain: it would enable our children to give God the praise He deserves for the prayers He has answered.

Prayer Posters

A few years ago, our friends Dennis and Donna, who pastor a neighboring church on Capitol Hill, told us about something God had impressed on them to do for their children. They identified words that were *descriptive* and *prescriptive* of their kids, had these words framed, and hung them on the walls in their rooms. They often wondered whether those words meant anything, but their oldest daughter, who is grown up and no longer living in their home, recently told them that some nights, when she hadn't been able to fall asleep, she would look at those words on the wall, and they would speak to her. Those framed words started to frame her. She started to see herself in the light of her God-ordained identity and destiny.

Lora and I loved the idea so much that we adapted it for Summer. Prior to Summer's thirteenth birthday, Lora recruited two of Summer's aunts to help her come up with a list of prophetic words to speak into Summer's life. Each of them took three words and discussed them with Summer over a special birthday dinner. We had a graphic designer turn those nine words into a poster. Each word is rendered in a different font, and these different fonts represent nine different dimensions of her identity, her destiny. These nine words are nine prayers that we'll pray for Summer for the rest of her life. It's a prayer list with a creative twist. Sometimes I'll go into Summer's room and use the poster as my prayer list. I also keep a picture of it on my phone.

Lunch Box Notes

Our friends Brad and Angie developed an interesting adaptation of this idea that they call lunch box notes. Like many parents, Angie dreaded the daily drudgery of packing brown-bag lunches for their three kids, so she decided to redeem the task. At first she looked for notes from stationery stores, but all she found was "You're a rock star" or "You're the coolest cat in class."

Angie decided to buy a pack of sticky notes instead and started writing scriptures, promises, and prayers to put in her kids' lunches. If one of the kids had an exam, she would circle a scripture like Psalm 121:2, which says, "My help comes from the

Lord." Sometimes she wrote down a challenge: "If you see someone in need, be the first person to help."

One of the keys to prayer is speaking in the language your kids understand. If their native tongue is texting, then you need to send texts at different times of the day and let them know you are circling them in prayer. But no matter what medium you use, praying circles around your children begins by identifying and specifying the promises you are believing God for.

A Book of Prayers

A few years ago, our friends Chris and Lora came up with what I thought was a brilliant idea. I'm not sure where it originated, but Chris and Lora asked family and friends to write out a prayer for their first son, Torin, while they were pregnant. They did the same thing for their second son, Declan. Then they bound that collection of prayers together and created a prayer book.

Each of those prayers is a prophecy delivered

through the personality of family and friends. And the simple fact that those prayers were written down makes it even more powerful and memorable. I can only imagine the moment when Chris and Lora give the prayer books to their sons. Seeing the prayers that were prayed for them before they were even born will flood their hearts with awe at the faithfulness of God.

I love the idea of putting together a prayer book before a baby is even born, but it's never too late. You can do it before the first day of kindergarten or after the last day of high school. You can even make it a wedding gift.

Life Goal List

Let me share one more practical way to make a prayer list: create a life goal list with your children.

Before Parker turned twelve, I spent several months designing a yearlong discipleship covenant that included a physical, an intellectual, and a spiritual component. The physical challenge was running a sprint triathlon together. The intellectual component was reading a dozen books together. And the spiritual component was multidimensional: we read through the New Testament and fasted from television during Lent. I also helped Parker craft his first life goal list. This list is in the *Student Edition* of *The Circle Maker,* a book he coauthored with me. While life goals might not strike you as being super-spiritual, I've found that my life goal list doubles as a prayer list, because I see each goal is an expression of faith. After all, faith is being sure of what we hope for (Hebrews 11:1). A goal will get you praying and keep you praying. It will also keep your relationships from becoming static. Nothing is more bonding than praying with your children, but right next to praying is playing. And playing doesn't end when your kids stop playing Candyland. One of the best ways to bond with your kids is by going after a shared goal.

In *The Circle Maker,* I share my personal list of 113 life goals. I came up with my first life goal list in my late twenties, but I've radically revised it since then. To be honest, my original list was rather selfish. It revolved around me, myself, and I. But I've since revised my list and added a relational component to almost every goal. So I no longer just want to visit the Eiffel Tower in Paris; I want to kiss my wife on top of it.

In the previous chapter, I talked about the importance of being a student of your children. One expression of that is designing a life goal list that reflects your children's unique interests. Summer is an exceptional swimmer, so one of my goals is to *Swim the Escape from Alcatraz* with her. She also loves musicals and New York City, so *Seeing a Broadway Play with Summer* made more sense than seeing *Mary Poppins* with one of my boys! Parker has my adventure gene, so several of my life goals reflect that. We checked two of them off the list while we were in Peru: we *Hiked the Inca Trail to Machu Picchu* and went *Paragliding over the Sacred Valley*. Josiah is a football fan, so when I got a chance to *Go to a Super Bowl*, I took him with me. And it just so happened that Super Bowl XLV coincided with his ninth birthday!

Chapter 6

The 3rd Circle:
Creating Prayer Mantras

*"When you pray, don't babble on and
on as people of other religions do."*

MATTHEW 6:7 NLT

During my yearlong discipleship covenant with Parker, we identified four core values that we want to define the Batterson family: *Gratitude, Humility, Generosity*, and *Courage*. We then translated each word into its Latin counterpart and turned them into a coat of arms that hangs in our house. Those four values are like the four points of a compass: they keep our family oriented. If you have never identified your family's core values or created a coat of arms, I'd highly recommend doing so.

Along with those core values, we have some mantras that we've picked up over the years from a wide variety of sources. By *mantras*, I simply mean sayings that get repeated over and over again. They are truisms that we want to serve as touchstones for our children. And if you repeat them often enough, those truths will get integrated in your child's way of thinking and way of life. With each repetition, the truth moves from the head closer to the heart and the conscience.

One of our most commonly quoted mantras is "Your focus determines your reality." That's what Qui-Gon Jinn said to Anakin Skywalker in *Star Wars: Episode I—The Phantom Menace.* It's what we say to our kids whenever they are in a funk. This mantra is a reminder to refocus on things that are good and right and pure and just, à la Philippians 4:8. It's a reminder that we don't see the world as it is; we see the world as we are. If you have a bad eye, you can find something wrong with anything. But if you have a good eye, you can always find something to give thanks for, something to praise God for.

Another Batterson mantra is "Remember the slide." That's what I say whenever our kids are afraid to try something new. It's a reference to a huge, hundred-foot-high slide at Cox Farms that terrified Josiah when he was younger. It took my most brilliant parental persuasion speech to get him to finally ride it. And by *brilliant persuasion speech,* I simply mean that I bribed him with candy if he would hop on a burlap bag and ride it with me tandem-style. He was absolutely terrified at the top, but thoroughly thrilled by the time we got to the bottom. I discerned a teachable moment, so I told my son that if we don't face our fears, we can miss out on a ton of fun. Then almost like a hypnotist employing an induction technique, I said to my son: "Remember the slide!" And I repeat it anytime Josiah needs to face a fear!

Another one of my favorite family mantras is a "deep thought" by American humorist Jack Handey: "If you drop your keys into a river of molten lava, let 'em go man 'cause they're gone."[8] I don't even have to quote the whole thing anymore. All I have to say is "If you drop your keys..." It's a reminder to let go and let God. It's a reminder to forgive and forget.

Prayer Mantras

We have a natural tendency to *remember what we should forget* and *forget what we should remember.*

That's where mantras come in. They serve as reminders of *who we are* and *what we're about* as a family. And no mantras are more important than prayer mantras. I have a few of them that I pray repeatedly as a pastor. Before preaching, for instance, I often pray, "Lord, help me help people." It's my way of simply submitting myself to God and asking Him to speak through me.

The most powerful prayer mantras are biblical, and the best example may be the Lord's Prayer. Of course, Jesus never meant it to become an empty incantation that we simply recite from memory. But if you actually pray it from the heart, the Lord's Prayer is powerful because you are praying the very words that Jesus Himself prescribed. You can pray with confidence when you are praying the *Word* of God because you know that it's the *will* of God. As you read through the Bible, certain words, phrases, or verses will jump off the page and into your spirit. The ones you circle over and over again will become your prayer mantras.

There is something powerful about a single

God-inspired prayer repeated throughout a child's lifetime. I've already mentioned a few of my prayer mantras, but the most significant one for our family is Luke 2:52: "May you grow 'in wisdom and stature and in favor with God and with man.'" Not long ago, Josiah came home from school super excited. He said, "Dad, you know that verse you pray for me every day? We read it in school today." He was beaming from ear to ear. It made my day because I could tell that the promise we've circled thousands of times is hardwired into his heart. He owns that promise, and that promise owns him!

Do I ever give this prayer mantra new language? Yes. I pray for God's favor on my kids in the classroom and on the court. I pray for His favor when my kids are applying for jobs and applying for schools. I pray that God will anoint their right brains and give them God ideas. And I pray that God will open doors of opportunity. So I pray in lots of different ways, but more often than not, I repeat the same prayer mantra so it gets engraved on their souls.

Three Simple Steps

So how do you create your own prayer mantras?

Here are three simple steps to get you started:

First of all, *pray about what to pray about.*

This is the first objective of prayer. The purpose of prayer is not to outline *our agenda for God*; the purpose is to get into the presence of God so we can be aligned with *God's agenda for us.* If you ask Him, God will reveal what He wants you to pray for your kids. I'd encourage you to make the mantra something that is memorable, but that doesn't mean it has to rhyme like a rap. The key is discerning God's heart for your children.

Second, *ask your kids questions.*

At different ages and stages, kids guard their deepest thoughts and strongest emotions like they're the gold at Fort Knox. Questions are the way you pick the lock. Jesus was the quintessential Question Asker. The gospels record 183 questions (depending upon your translation). With one well-crafted question, Jesus had the ability to define situations, resolve conflict, and reveal motivations. My tendency is to preach at my kids when we have a disagreement, but that often causes our kids to clam up even more. But a well-timed question can open sesame. When they are young, it can be as simple as asking them to share the highlight and lowlight of their day. When they get older, ask them their opinion on issues. You might not agree with their teenage logic every time, but your question will show them that you value what they think and open up the lines of communications. In addition, their answers to your questions are clues that will help lead you to the right prayer mantras.

Third, *go back to the Bible.*

Don't just read it. If all you do is read the Bible, then you are actually *misreading* it. The Bible wasn't meant to be read; it was meant to be prayed. Reading is how you get through the Bible, but praying is how you get the Bible through you. When you start reading, ask the Holy Spirit to speak to you. The same Holy Spirit who inspired the original writers wants to illuminate readers. And in my experience, He will do it by quickening certain words and phrases and promises. They'll jump off the page and into your spirit. That's when you need to stop reading and start praying those things for your children. Then you simply pick back up wherever you left off and keep praying your way through the Bible.

A Proverbs 31 Woman

Remember when Samuel went out looking for the next king of Israel, and David's father, Jesse, didn't even bother to call David in from the fields? David's own dad didn't see who he could or would become. When Jesse looked at David, he saw a shepherd boy. But when the prophet Samuel looked at David, he saw a king (1 Samuel 16:1–13).

One of the great dangers of family relationships is that we become blind to the beauty and mystery all around us simply because we live in such close proximity to it.

You need a vision for your children.

With your physical eyes, you *see who a person is*.

With your spiritual eyes, you *see what that person can become.* And it's when you close your physical eyes in prayer that God will open your spiritual eyes to perceive what is far more real than the reality you can perceive with your five senses.

One reader of *The Circle Maker* wrote to tell me that he is praying that his two daughters become Proverbs 31 women. When he first started praying this prayer, his oldest daughter asked him what it meant. He told her to read it, study it, and pray about it herself. As she does so, she is discovering her divine destiny. After all, Scripture is a mirror that enables her to see who she really is in Christ. And Proverbs 31 is a beautiful reflection of what it means to be a woman of God. So every night this father prays that his daughters will become Proverbs 31 women. One night when he forgot to include this prayer mantra, his youngest daughter reminded him: "Daddy, you forgot to say that we would be Proverbs 31 women!" That's when you know the prayer mantra is working!

I got another e-mail from a reader whose son wasn't inherently cheerful or particularly obedient, but that is what he felt led to pray for. After years of praying that his son would be cheerful and obedient, this father saw his son's disposition radically change. Those prayers were prophecies! They created new tendencies and capacities within his son.

One of my prayer mantras for Summer is that she will one day marry someone who *loves God more than he loves her.* If her future spouse seeks God's face more than he seeks my daughter's hand, I have zero concerns about their future together. I will pray this prayer for Summer until the day I walk her down the aisle. Someday I'll ask the question of whatever young man asks for my daughter's hand in marriage: "Do you love God more than you love my daughter?" If the answer is yes, that young man will have my blessing.

Praying for Future Spouses

We only make a few major decisions in life. Then we spend the rest of our lives managing those major decisions. And the biggest one besides choosing

Christ is choosing a spouse. So while it's difficult to pray for someone you may not know yet, praying for your child's future spouse has the potential to pay huge dividends. In the words of Psalm 102:18, "Let this be recorded for a generation to come, so that a people yet to be created may praise the LORD" (ESV).

I'm eternally grateful for a mother-in-law and father-in-law who interceded for me long before I met their daughter, Lora. And I want to follow suit. On my children's wedding days, I want to be able to say that I was praying for my son-in-law or daughter-in-law long before they ever met my son or daughter! I want them to know that they are an answer to prayer—literally!

My friend Wayne started praying for his child's future spouse during the early stages of his wife's pregnancy. Every evening Wayne would lay hands on Diane's stomach and pray the promises in Scripture that they had circled for their baby. Then he came across a book that said it was never too early to start praying for their baby's future spouse, so they added that to their prayer list. At first it seemed odd to pray for a spouse before they even knew the gender of their baby. In fact, they didn't know if their baby's future spouse was even born yet! But they prayed for their baby and their baby's spouse day after day until their due date.

Wayne and Diane had decided to wait until the birth to discover their baby's gender, but they prayed that God would reveal what the baby's name should be. In October of 1983, the Lord gave them a girl's name—Jessica. Then in December, the Lord gave them a boy's name—Timothy. They weren't sure why God had given them two different names because they weren't having twins, but they prayed circles around Jessica and Timothy until Diane gave birth.

On May 5, 1984, God answered their prayers when Diane gave birth to a baby boy they named Timothy. Wayne and Diane continued to circle their son in prayer, but they also kept praying for the girl that he would one day marry. Twenty-two years and two weeks of accumulated prayers culminated on May 19, 2006. That is the day Timothy's bride walked down the aisle. Her name? Jessica.

Here's the rest of the story.

Their future daughter-in-law was born on October 19, 1983—the same month that God gave them the name Jessica. A thousand miles away, Wayne and Diane were praying for her by name. They thought Jessica would be their daughter, not their daughter-in-law, but God always has a surprise up His sovereign sleeve. God gave Wayne and Diane two promises, two miracles, two names.

In case you're wondering, Timothy was allowed to date girls who weren't named Jessica! Wayne and Diane didn't tell Timothy that God had given them the name of his future spouse before he was born until after he and Jessica were engaged.

A Time-Stamped Letter

Second Corinthians 3:3 says: "You are a letter from Christ."

The ramifications of that one statement are profound. You may be the only Bible some people ever read. So the question is: Are you a good translation? While we each translate the gospel through our unique personality, passions, and professions, the Author of our salvation wants to tell His-story through our lives and the lives of our children. Our kids are time-stamped letters to the next generation. And one key to creating prayer mantras is identifying their unique storylines.

Our destiny is buried in our history. If you look closely, you'll discover clues that are cues. Architects built cities out of Legos. Saleswomen sold enough Thin Mint Girl Scout cookies to feed a small country. And entrepreneurs cornered the lemonade stand market on their cul-de-sacs. And while children are often oblivious to the future-tense ramifications of their present-tense interests, parents must function as destiny detectives.

As English playwright Graham Greene insightfully observed, "There is always one moment in childhood when the door opens and lets the future in."

For me, the door opened during a sophomore speech class. I gave what amounted to a salvation sermon as my final project. I don't think any of my classmates got saved, but that speech became an inciting incident in my storyline. Unbeknownst to me, my mom gave a copy of that speech to my grandma who gave a copy to her Bible study teacher. The teacher asked my grandma, "Has Mark ever thought about ministry?" At that point in my story, the answer was no. It hadn't even crossed my mind until that question was relayed from my grandma to my mom to me. My mom and grandma saw something in me that I didn't see in myself. And they didn't just see it in me. They called it out of me.

That's what prophets do; that's what parents do.

For better or for worse, transition points are often turning points in the lives our children. So at critical junctures, they need well-planned and well-prayed words of wisdom. You might want to design a discipleship covenant before their thirteenth birthday. Or put your life lessons on paper and give it to them as a graduation present—along with something of monetary value, of course! Or send them off to college with a token of your faith in them. As you circle your kids and grandkids during those transitions, the Holy Spirit will lead you in leveraging those key times for His purposes.

Storylines

As prophet-historians, our job is to help our children identify their storylines. Those storylines are expressions of their soulprint, their true identity and destiny in Christ.

I often reference Parker's adventure gene or Summer's ability to light up a room or Josiah's heart that is sensitized to the Holy Spirit. We can't just catch our kids doing things wrong. We have to catch them doing things right. Then we need to celebrate those things that we see in them. That's how we help our children discover their spiritual sweet spot—that place where their God-given gifts and God-ordained passions overlap.

One of my professors in graduate school put it this way: "What makes you cry or pound your fist on the table?" In other words, what makes you sad or mad? That is a God-ordained passion you need to pursue. I would simply add *glad* to the mix. In the words of American writer and theologian Frederick Buechner,

> The voice we should listen to most as we choose a vocation is the voice that we might think we should listen to least, and that is the voice of our own gladness. What can we do that makes us the gladdest, what can we do that leaves us with the strongest sense of sailing true north and of peace, which is much of what gladness is? I believe that if it is a thing that makes us truly glad, then it is a good thing and it is our thing.[9]

What is your child's thing? What makes them laugh? What makes them cry? What ticks them off or lights them up? If we want to help them discover their destiny, we need to follow their trail of tears and echoes of laughter.

As God reveals your children's life themes, you

may want to consider coupling them with a life verse. I don't think you want to do this lightly. And I'm certainly not suggesting that you emphasize one verse to the exclusion of others. But God will give you different verses for different seasons. Two of my prayer mantras for Josiah during this life stage are that he would be "strong and courageous" and do what is "right in the eyes of the LORD" (Joshua 1:9; 1 Kings 15:5; and many other verses). Those prayers are prophecies. And if we keep circling those life verses, they will eventually become life themes.

Chapter 7

The 4th Circle:
Praying a Hedge of Protection

And we know that in all things God works
for the good of those who love him, who have
been called according to his purpose.

ROMANS 8:28

When our children were about waist-high, our family vacationed at a friend's cabin in Deep Creek, Maryland. It was nestled in a densely wooded area where we wouldn't have been surprised to bump into Bigfoot. And while there hadn't been any Sasquatch sightings, we were warned that hungry brown bears would show up every now and then looking for leftovers. Late one night, I decided to get into the hot tub with Parker and Summer. It was cold and snowy, so steam was rising from the hot tub. And it was pitch-black because the trees formed a canopy that blocked the moonlight. All we could hear were the sounds of the forest, and that combination of factors put our nerve endings on red alert. Translation: the kids were downright scared. And—truth be told—so was I.

As we soaked in the 104-degree water, my

protective impulses boiled over. In an overly dramatic voice, I made a fatherly proclamation to my children: "If a bear came out of these woods and attacked us, I would die for you." For the record, our kids were six and eight at the time. Let's just say that my words were far from reassuring. Parker and Summer jumped out of the hot tub and ran into the house screaming. It's a miracle they aren't scared and scarred to this day!

I probably should have handled my pronouncement differently, but I meant what I said with every fiber of my being. I would die for my children without a moment's hesitation under any circumstances! It was the purest and strongest concentration of protective instincts I've ever felt. And I believe that is a healthy and holy instinct—a mirror image of our heavenly Father. You are the apple of His eye. And anyone who messes with you messes with Him. His protective instincts are most poignantly seen on the cross. That's where the Advocate took His stand against the Accuser of the brethren. That's where the sinless Son of God took the fall for fallen sinners.

Remember the story of the woman caught in

the act of adultery? It's one of my favorite stories because Jesus' protective instincts are on full display. He defended this woman as if she were His daughter or sister. He stood between this woman and the men who were ready to stone her to death. Jesus Himself acted as the hedge of protection. When He said, "Let any one of you who is without sin be the first to throw a stone at her" (John 8:7), it was His way of saying, "You can stone her over My dead body!"

As a parent, I am called to be a provider for and a protector of my family, and I believe in praying a hedge of protection around my children. But let me offer a word of caution as well. When we're overprotective as parents it can be counterproductive for our children. Sometimes we need to get out of the way of what God wants to do.

Nonintervention

One of the hardest lessons to learn as a parent, especially if you're a "helicopter parent" who hovers around your children, is that kids actually need to fall down and skin their knees so they learn how to get back up and dust themselves off. If you always intervene, it's like helping a caterpillar escape its cocoon too quickly and easily, thereby crippling its wings. Your efforts to help your kids might actually hurt them. Sometimes tough love means letting them serve the detention, pay the fine, or even spend a night in jail. If you bail them out of every financial mess they get into, they'll never learn the value of a dollar. I'm certainly not suggesting that there aren't moments when we should show our kids amazing grace. But if you always interrupt the consequences of their actions, you short-circuit the full development of their conscience. I know it's awfully hard to hold back your hand, but that's how your kids learn to hold the hand of God.

My daughter, Summer, recently went on a mission trip to Zambia that cost $2,900. She managed to raise $2,200, but that's when all of her fund-raising efforts dried up. Two days before the trip, I was tempted to leverage my social networks on her behalf to simply bail her out with an "anonymous" gift. But I felt a check. If I had intervened, I would have robbed God of an opportunity to reveal Himself as Jehovah Jireh. The day before her mission trip, Summer went to the bank to withdraw every penny she'd earned at her summer job to cover the balance of her trip. Right after executing the withdrawal, she checked her mission's account online and was shocked to discover that several last-minute donors had completely paid for her trip in its entirety! If I had intervened, I would have interfered with God's miraculous provision.

I'm more and more convinced that we're all control freaks and children are God's cure. And if you have lots of control issues, you might need lots of kids! You might be able to maintain a measure of control when they are young, but just wait until they get their licenses. Teenagers are the cure-all for control issues.

Double Bind

I believe God can keep things from happening. That's why I pray for traveling mercies, especially since

Parker has gotten his license. And when Summer was in Zambia on her mission trip, I constantly prayed a hedge of protection around her! That's my prerogative as a parent. But one of the common mistakes we make as parents is only praying defensively. There's nothing wrong with praying that God would keep our kids safe, but we also need to pray that God would make them dangerous! Don't just pray a hedge of protection; pray that they would courageously invade enemy territory with the light and love of Jesus.

In psychology, there is a concept called the double bind. If I tell you to *be spontaneous*, you can't *be spontaneous* precisely because I just told you to be! I think we do the same thing with sin. If you simply tell someone, "Don't sin," you put that person in a spiritual double bind. Let me explain. You can't stop sinning by not sinning. You can't *run away* from sin without *running toward* God. Fleeing sin and seeking God are two sides of the same coin.

The cure for sin is *not* not sinning. The cure for sin is a vision from God that is bigger and better than your sinful desires. So don't just pray that your kids' hearts won't be broken by a boyfriend or girlfriend; pray that their hearts will break for the things that break the heart of God. One of the quickest ways to accomplish that is to send your kids on a mission trip. It'll put their first-world problems in perspective! And if God gets a hold of their heart, it will wreck them for anything less than God's good, pleasing, and perfect will (Romans 12:2).

Plead the Blood

The devil knows how to hit us where it hurts most—our children. Make no mistake: there is a target on their backs. And the enemy isn't afraid of hitting below the belt. If he can't take you out, he'll go after your kids. That doesn't mean we need to live in fear. After all, the enemy has already been defeated. But we do need to be aware of the enemy's schemes.

Just like the blood over the doorposts that protected the children of Israel on the Passover, the blood of Jesus provides a protective covering for us.

The enemy has no jurisdiction in your life. You can do more than resist the devil; you can rebuke Him the way Jesus did. But you have to plead the blood of Jesus and stay on your knees. And you need to teach your children about spiritual warfare. They need to know that God loves them and has a wonderful plan for their lives, but they also need to know that the enemy hates them and has a horrible plan for their lives. And the choice is theirs!

So don't forget who your fight is with! If you do, you'll fight *with* your kids instead of fighting *for* them. Our battle is not with our strong-willed toddler or rebellious teenager no matter what they've done wrong. Our only enemy is an ancient foe named Satan. And the way we wage war with him is on our knees. Prayer is the difference between *you fighting for God* and *God fighting for you*. Let God fight your battles for you! And remember, you're not the Holy Spirit. You can certainly confront your children when they do something wrong, but only the Holy Spirit can bring the conviction that leads to confession. That's His job, not yours.

The Terminator

In her book *Girls with Swords*, Lisa Bevere likens the enemy's attacks to the 1984 science-fiction film *The Terminator*, starring Arnold Schwarzenegger. It's the story of a waitress named Sarah Connor living a rather routine life until a robotic assassin from the year 2029 tries to terminate her. At the same time, a protector named Kyle Reese intervenes to save her life.

Sarah isn't sure why the Terminator is targeting her until Reese explains that, in the near future, an artificial intelligence defense network called Skynet will become self-aware and initiate a nuclear holocaust designed to wipe out mankind. Sarah's yet-to-be-born son, John Connor, will rally the survivors and lead a resistance movement against Skynet and its army of machines. With the Resistance on the verge of victory, Skynet has sent a Terminator back in time to kill Sarah before John can be born as a last-ditch effort to avert the formation of the Resistance.

Can I take this opportunity to make an observation?

You may believe in your child more than anyone on this planet, but you still underestimate what they can accomplish for the kingdom of God. Your child might write a film script or a book that causes a seismic shift in culture. They might find the cure for cancer that saves your life or start a business that funds kingdom causes in third-world countries. You may be raising a pastor who will someday lead a city-changing church, or you may be raising the future leader of the free world.

I love Lisa Bevere's take on *The Terminator* as an archetypal character of the one who comes to kill, steal, and destroy: "The attacks on your life have much more to do with who you might be in the future than who you have been in the past."[10]

The enemy doesn't know the future any more than we do, but he knows how to target those with tremendous future potential, aka our children. Just like Jochebed, the mother of Moses who hid her son in a basket made of bulrushes, we need to spot those schemes and take proactive measures. We need to do everything within our power to not just protect our children from the enemy's schemes but also to catapult them into their God-ordained destiny. If Jochebed hadn't done what she did, Moses would have either been killed or grown up as a slave. But because of his mother's prophetic foresight, Moses was raised in Pharaoh's palace.

The most powerful thing we can do as parents is plead the blood of Jesus over our children. And you never know, their salvation might just lead to the salvation of an entire nation just as it did for Moses and the people of Israel. But like Jochebed, you—and they—might have to endure some suffering before the salvation.

Why, God?

My friends John and Tricia Tiller experienced a parent's worst nightmare nearly a decade ago when their three-year-old son fell out of a second-story-bedroom window. Eli was medevaced to the hospital, where he fought for his life in the ICU for three weeks. He miraculously survived, but not without significant brain damage. He has virtually no peripheral vision on his right side, and the left side of his body has very little motor skills or muscle development. Eli speaks with a severe stutter and walks with a pronounced limp. Yet Eli, who is now twelve years old, has as sweet a spirit and as courageous an attitude as anybody I've ever met. John recently shared their story at National Community Church, and Eli sang a rendition of Chris Tomlin's song "I Will Rise." There wasn't a dry eye in the house! It's worth watching on YouTube. Or, better yet, invite them to share their testimony at your church.

John and Tricia have thanked God countless times for saving their son, but their prayers for complete healing have gone unanswered. In the aftermath of the accident, John dueled with doubt as any normal dad would:

> I began to interrogate God. "Why, God? Why do little boys fall from windows?" Why did my little

boy fall from that window? Why him? Why me? I looked to Scripture for an answer, and it turns out that "Why, God?" is not a new question at all.

In John 9, Jesus encountered a man who was born blind. His friends and family assumed that his disability was the result of some kind of disobedience. They asked Jesus, "Who sinned, this man or his parents?" (v. 2). But Jesus debunked their false assumption. The people assumed it was a generational curse or a lack of faith, but Jesus set the record straight by revealing the real reason: "This happened so that the works of God might be displayed in him" (v. 3).

Let me ask you a couple point-blank questions: What is your deepest desire and highest hope for your children? Is it that your children will glorify God and serve His purpose in their generation? If it is, then you have to come to terms with the fact that while God can put a hedge of protection around your children, sometimes suffering is part of the sanctification process in their lives. I'm not suggesting that God causes it, but He can redeem it. He recycles our pain for other people's gain. Nothing is more painful for parents than watching their children suffer, and I'm not suggesting that we don't do everything within our power to protect them and help them, but there are some lessons that can only be learned through a graduate course in pain and suffering. And it might mean that God has greater plans and purposes for their lives than what we're aware of.

Praying Through the Problem

Since Eli Tiller's accident, John and Tricia have done everything humanly possible to help their son. They've spent tens of thousands of dollars on medical equipment not covered by insurance. For the three years following the accident, Tricia and Eli spent 80 percent of their waking hours in therapy. They had faith that Eli would be completely healed, so they prayed and waited. Then they waited and prayed. But after three years of holding out hope for his complete healing, they felt that it was time to accept Eli's condition and choose to live life with disability.

In John's words,

> We had to burn our old scripts and look for what God could do with our new script. So for the past five years, we've accepted life with disability. That doesn't mean I've stopped praying for my son. Like any father, I'd give my right arm to see my son healed. But instead of getting discouraged or getting angry, I choose to look for what God can do.

If we're being completely honest, most of our prayers have as their chief objective our own personal comfort rather than God's glory. We try to pray away every problem, but those shortsighted prayers would short-circuit God's perfect plan. So don't try to pray away the problem until you've learned the lesson God is trying to teach you. Remember, the primary purpose of prayer is not to change our circumstances.

The primary purpose is to change us, to change our children. More than anything, I want my children to be conformed to the image of Christ. And that means I sometimes need to pray *get them through* versus *get them out* prayers! Instead of praying away our problems, we need to pray through them.

Praying a hedge of protection around your children isn't praying for the path of least resistance. And it doesn't shield them from the challenges that God will use to build their character. It's praying for the path that will lead to God's greatest glory, and that path has potholes called pain. But God can protect them from the plots of the evil one. As parents, we stand on the promise that God will work all things together for the good of those who love Him and are called according to His purpose (Romans 8:28). God will turn their temporary pain into eternal gain. And that's the reward we're after.

Chapter 8

The 5th Circle:
Forming Prayer Circles

*Don't let anyone look down on you
because you are young, but set an
example for the believers in speech, in
conduct, in love, in faith and in purity.*

1 TIMOTHY 4:12

While her husband was a professor at the University of Pennsylvania, pastor and speaker Tony Campolo's wife was a stay-at-home mom. At faculty functions, Peggy would invariably get asked what she did, and when she revealed that she was a full-time mom, she often felt patronized by the intelligentsia who seemed to think her role in society was somehow less significant than theirs. That's when she decided to redefine her role. The next time an unsuspecting academic asked her what she did, Peggy translated it into terminology they could appreciate. She said,

> I am socializing two Homo Sapiens in the dominant values of the Judeo-Christian tradition in order that they might be instruments

for the transformation of the social order into the teleologically prescribed utopia inherent in the eschaton.

After a brief pause, she said, "And what is it that you do?"

That ranks as one of my all-time favorite definitions of parenting! And don't feel bad if you need a dictionary: I had to look up a few words too!

There is no greater privilege than parenting. It's our highest calling, and there isn't a close second. But if you think you can pull it off all by yourself, you're fooling yourself. Of course you aren't fooling your kids! Kids seem to instinctively know how to divide and conquer Mom and Dad to get what they want.

God knew we'd need to double-team our kids on occasion, so He designed the family unit with a mom and a dad. For the record, I have high esteem for single parents who essentially take on the job of both. They're like the two-way athlete who plays offense and defense with no timeouts.

Learning to Lean

Before we zoom in on forming prayer circles, let me zoom out and take a little pressure off of you.

First of all, healthy parents learn to lean on their spouse's strengths. Of course, that means you need to discover those strengths first. I would highly recommend taking the Myers-Briggs personality instrument. Few things have been more revealing for our marriage or parenting styles. For the record, Lora and I are exact opposites. And while that can cause an occasional conflict, it has helped us parent our children more holistically. When our kids want a sleepover or some spending money, they usually ask me because I have a harder time saying no. But Lora and I have learned that it's not fair to her if she has to play bad cop all the time! Simply being aware of our strengths and weaknesses has helped us both complement and appreciate each other. We've had to discover who's better suited to teach a new skill or help with homework or take them for driving practice. Of course I think it's critically important for both parents—regardless of personality type—to be involved in rewarding positive behavior and disciplining negative behavior.

Beyond Mom and Dad, one key to parenting is learn to lean on extended family. I know that in our highly transient society that isn't a luxury everybody has. But there are still ways to engage grandparents even if they don't live down the block. A highlight of the year, every year, is our kids spending a week with Grandpa and Grandma Batterson in Florida. And even though they live a thousand miles away, I covet their prayers for our kids! We're also fortunate to have Lora's side of the family living in close proximity, and no one makes a better babysitter than a crazy aunt or uncle! These aunts and uncles have also become spiritual confidants for our kids.

I'm profoundly grateful for our biological family, but I'm also grateful for our spiritual family. As I've already stated, it's not the job of youth pastors to disciple my kids. That's my job. But I'm so grateful that I have someone to tag-team with. Whether it's going to a game, grabbing a meal, or intentional discipleship, those mentoring moments are priceless investments in my kids. Along with mentors who have taken my kids under their wings, we also have a team of prayer partners at National Community Church who intercede for us Battersons every day. And my kids are at the top of that list.

As parents, we need all of the above!

The Laying On of Hands

Drawing prayer circles starts with the family circle. Sometimes we'll kneel as a family or hold hands, but my favorite is laying hands on my children while I pray for them. That physical connection creates a spiritual bond. And there is something mystical and powerful about following a biblical prescription to the letter of the law. There are lots of verses that reference the laying on of hands, and it can be done for a wide variety of reasons that range from healing to blessing. Jesus set the example for us in Matthew 19:

One day some parents brought their children to Jesus so he could lay his hands on them and pray for them. But the disciples scolded the parents for bothering him.

But Jesus said, "Let the children come to me. Don't stop them! For the Kingdom of Heaven belongs to those who are like these children." And he placed his hands on their heads and blessed them before he left. (vv. 13–15 NLT)

A few years ago, during a family devotion, I felt prompted to have our family physically circle Josiah. Then I put my hands on his chest and prayed for my son. Actually, I felt like I was praying *into* him. It was as if the physical contact created a conduit between my son and me. I felt like the Holy Spirit put a prayer in my heart, so I boldly declared it: "Lord, let Josiah grow into the destiny of his name." As you may have guessed, Josiah is named after an ancient Jewish king whose spiritual exploits were many but are summarized in one mantra: "He did what was right in the eyes of the Lord." As I prayed that prayer, I was declaring Josiah's destiny.

Later that night, after brushing his teeth and putting on his pajamas, Josiah innocently said, "Dad, I can't wait to grow up to be a king." Slight misinterpretation of my prayer! Lora asked me if I corrected him. Nope. Didn't have the heart.

Then Josiah said something that helped me appreciate an ancient biblical ritual in a way that no theologian could teach me. He said, "Dad, have you done that hands thing with Parker and Summer?" Josiah didn't have the theological terminology down pat or fully understand the biblical precedent, but he thought the laying on of hands was the coolest thing in the world. And it is. But it's more than that; it creates a spiritual bond between parent and child.

The Power of Touch

When parents brought their children to be blessed by Jesus, He put His hands on their head. Why don't we follow suit? One way to stay in touch with our children is to . . . touch them! Give them a bear hug or a pat on the back. Put your hand on their head when you pray. Touch creates a touchstone for your kids and you.

Research has shown that touch has the power to fight viruses, relieve stress, improve sleep, and help us recover more quickly from injury. One study done by a group of Utah researchers found that a thirty-minute massage three times a week lowers levels of the stress-related enzyme alpha-amylase by 34 percent.[11] You may want to underline this last sentence and put it on your spouse's nightstand.

The power of touch, even on a physical level, is an amazing thing. But when you add the power of God to the equation, touch sets the stage for something supernatural to happen. The biblical practice of the laying on of hands is an endangered practice in many church circles. We don't do it for a wide range of reasons. Maybe the church you grew up in didn't do it, or it feels a little too close for comfort. Whatever the reason, the net result can be a lack of faith, a lack of miracles, and a lack of deliverance.

Call me a simpleton, but I believe that if we simply do what the people in the Bible did, we may experience what they experienced. Who knows how many miraculous moments we've forfeited because we've failed to act in a bold, biblical fashion by praying for someone who is sick, commissioning someone who is called, or encouraging someone who just needs a hand on his or her shoulder? And bold prayers ought to start in the home with our children.

Praying With vs. Praying For

One reason I love the story of King Josiah is that he was only eight years old when he assumed the throne.

Too often we let age be an excuse, but you're never too young or too old to be used by God. King Josiah didn't let his youthfulness keep him from calling a nation to bend its knees. Whatever you do, don't underestimate your children's potential. Give them opportunities to exercise their spiritual gifts, and they just might surprise you.

Great parenting doesn't only mean *teaching your children;* it also means *learning from them.* Think of it as reverse mentoring. After all, Jesus said, "Unless you change and become like little children, you will never enter the kingdom of heaven" (Matthew 18:3).

When I'm in a place of spiritual desperation, I often ask my kids to pray. There is something uniquely powerful about children's prayers—and it's their childlike faith. Their faith hasn't been infected by logic yet. In *The Circle Maker,* I shared the story of an $8 million piece of property on Capitol Hill that our church owns debt-free. It took a miracle to get a contract on it, and I believe the genesis of that miracle was a simple prayer prayed by one of my children.

On the very day we thought we would sign a contract on that property, we lost the contract to a real estate development corporation. I felt defeated. I went home and asked our family to kneel in prayer. I had lost faith, but my kids had not. I'll never forget one of their straightforward prayers: "God, use that property for Your glory." It was so simple. It was so pure. It was so full of faith. Somehow that prayer resuscitated my faith, and I knew God would answer. And I honestly believe that's why we own it.

A Five-Year-Old's Prayers

I recently got an e-mail from the mother of a five-year-old boy named Ethan who might rank as the youngest reader of *The Circle Maker*. To be honest, I'd recommend the kids' edition of *The Circle Maker* for five-year-olds, but Ethan is an exception.

It all started one Sunday when Ethan stayed in the adult service at church instead of going to kids' church. Their church was doing a series on *The Circle Maker,* and the pastor told the story of Honi the Circle Maker. Ethan decided to draw his own prayer circle. The next day he announced to his mom: "I'm praying for a baby by Sunday or Monday." He was so convinced that Ethan even told his mom that she needed to get the nursery ready and pack her bags because they'd have to get the baby from the hospital.

Ethan's dad and mom, Ben and Mattie, had been praying for a baby as well. But their hearts had been broken and their faith had been shaken by the stillbirth of their daughter, Shyla Joy, and the miscarriage of their son, Jakin Isaac. Those two painful losses were followed by a failed adoption. A friend asked Ben and Mattie to adopt her baby, but after giving him a name and bringing him home, their friend changed her mind.

Despite being near the bottom of the adoption list, Mattie got an e-mail four days after Ethan's prayer that a newborn baby girl in the NICU needed a family. And because of unique circumstances, she needed a family the next day! If it had not been for Ethan's prayer, the long list of medical problems might have scared away Ben and Mattie. But despite an earthquake, a blizzard, a closed interstate, a canceled layover, and lost luggage, they arrived at the hospital on Sunday, November 11, 2012. Ethan's prayer—or maybe I should say *prophecy*—was fulfilled in a way that no one could have planned or predicted.

Ben and Mattie named their little girl Arabelle. It means "an answer to prayer." And that's exactly what she is. Arabelle is an answer to her big brother Ethan's prayers. And her complete healing and health are an answer to prayer as well.

Backseat Versus Driver's Seat

One of the most important lessons I've learned as a parent is that you cannot practice the spiritual disciplines *for* your kids. You have to practice them *with* your kids. Otherwise you will stunt their spiritual growth.

The day I turned sixteen, I went to the local Department of Motor Vehicles to get my license. I couldn't wait. I'll never forget the feeling of freedom as I sat behind the wheel for the first time: *I can go anywhere I want to.* That's when two things dawned on me. First, gas costs money! Second, I didn't know how to get anywhere! The crazy thing is that I had crisscrossed every square inch of my hometown—Naperville, Illinois—a thousand times. Why did I suddenly not know where to drive? Because I had been in the backseat, not the driver's seat. I hadn't been paying attention to where we were going or how we got there. I was just along for the ride.

The same is true spiritually. Until kids get into the driver's seat, they won't know how to get anywhere. What do I mean? You can pray *for* them their entire lives, but if you never let them pray, they're just along for the ride. They won't know how to get anywhere in prayer.

One of the greatest responsibilities of parenthood is praying for your kids, but an even greater responsibility is teaching your kids to pray. Don't just pray *for* them; pray *with* them. Praying *for* your kids is like taking them for a ride; praying *with* your kids is like teaching them to drive. If all you ever do is pray *for* your kids, they'll just stay in the backseat. Your kids will become spiritual codependents who ask you for a ride anytime they need to get somewhere spiritually. But if you teach them to pray, they can download directions themselves and make their way to wherever it is that God wants them to go.

Last year for Lent, Parker and I did a little prayer experiment—or, as I like to call it, an *experiLent*. We decided to get up at six o' clock on school days to give us a little extra time to pray together in the morning. We decided we would kneel in prayer. Then we took turns praying for each other. Was every prayer time amazing? No. In fact, I had to nudge Parker a time or two because my prayer put him to sleep! But we also had some powerful times kneeling in the presence of God before His throne. I'm not sure I can teach my children anything more important or more powerful than to kneel before God in prayer.

Aaron and Hur

After *The Circle Maker* was released, I embarked on a book tour that took me to a dozen cities in a span of ten weeks. I love book tours because I love connecting with readers in person, but these tours also take a toll. During that book tour, National Community Church was going through a significant growth spurt that demanded every ounce of creativity and energy I had. So between the speaking and pastoring, I was pretty well spent.

Right before one of those trips, I asked my family to pray for me. I'm usually on the praying end, but I needed to be on the receiving end. So I knelt down, and my wife and children laid hands on me. They took turns praying for me, and as they prayed, I could hardly keep from crying. I felt so loved, so empowered, so encouraged by that prayer circle. Then, after everyone had taken their turn and I thought they were done, Parker started praying again. This was no perfunctory prayer. I could tell the Holy Spirit had inspired him to add something to his earlier prayer. He put his hand on my back and prayed, "Lord, I pray that Pops would maintain his integrity and transparency during this stressful season."

When your own son prays that kind of prayer for you, it takes accountability to a whole new level. It was like the Holy Spirit steeled my resolve to live with integrity and transparency.

Remember the story of Aaron and Hur holding up the arms of Moses during battle? Moses had lost his strength, and when he lowered his arms, the Israelite army lost ground. But as long as Aaron and Hur lifted his arms, the army was victorious (Exodus 17:8–16).

All of us need Aarons and Hurs in our lives. We need people who are strong when we are weak.

We need people who are full of faith when we are running on empty. We need people who will fight for us on their knees. We all need a prayer circle!

Sometimes parents play the role of Aaron and Hur, but sometimes our children hold up our arms. I recently got an e-mail from a dad who had been unemployed for eight long months. He was angry with God and angry with himself. He had stopped leading family devotions because he felt like a failure on the job front. After reading *The Circle Maker*, he decided it was time to start again. He led his family in prayer for the first time in a long time. Then his wife and kids prayed for him. As his wife prayed, his children literally held up his arms, just as Aaron and Hur had done for Moses.

It was a moment that dad will never forget.

That's what families are for.

Chapter 9

The 6th Circle:
Praying Through the Bible

As the rain and the snow
come down from heaven,
and do not return to it
without watering the earth
and making it bud and flourish,
so that it yields seed for the sower and
bread for the eater,
so is my word that goes out from my mouth:
It will not return to me empty,
but will accomplish what I desire
and achieve the purpose for which I sent it.

ISAIAH 55:10–11

One of my most treasured possessions is a Bible that belonged to my Grandpa Johnson. I love seeing his notes in the margins. I love seeing which verses he underlined. Sometimes I'll even do my personal devotions out of his Bible.

I want to leave a similar legacy for my children. In fact, I want to give each of my children a Bible that was prayed through specifically for them. I recently got my hands on a Bible edition inspired by an idea that comes from Jonathan Edwards, the eighteenth-century theologian and pastor. Edwards loved writing notes while he read, so he hand-stitched blank pages into his Bible. In the Bible edition I have, every other page is blank, allowing me to write prayers and record thoughts for my children. I'll give each of them their own personal copy before they go off to college.

My friend Wayne has done the same thing for

his children. He prayed through the entire Bible with each of his children in mind, starting with his oldest son, Timothy. Wayne circled and underlined verses that were Timothy-specific. He wrote notes in the margins. He literally prayed every promise for his children. Then a few weeks before Timothy graduated from high school, Wayne planned a special event at a nearby restaurant—all of which was a complete surprise to his son. A handful of influencers in Timothy's life presented him with gifts. Wayne gave him the "finisher" medal from his third Marine Corps Marathon. But the most significant moment—and the most significant gift—came when Wayne gave Timothy the Bible. In Wayne's words, "My greatest joy is knowing I have prayed every word of God, every promise of God, with Timothy in mind." Wayne said it was one of the few times in his life when he saw grown men sobbing uncontrollably.

Now let's be honest. Our children don't always appreciate what we do for them at the moment when we do it. It's usually not until we have kids of our own that we appreciate the sacrifices our parents made for us. So don't be disappointed if you feel like your prayer circles aren't making a difference. But trust me: they are and they will. Or maybe you feel like it's too little, too late. Listen, it's never too late to be who you might have been. Or maybe your kids are already adults and you feel like you missed your opportunity. God gives us a second chance, and it's called *becoming a grandparent.* You can do for your grandchildren what you failed to do for your children.

Live Unoffended

My friends John and Heidi are part of my personal prayer circle, and God has given them some amazing answers to the prayers they've prayed for others, but many of their prayers for their own family have gone unanswered. A step of faith into the world of filmmaking resulted in the loss of their life savings when financial backing didn't materialize as promised. Their family had to move out of their home because of a fire. They lost three of their four parents in four years. And a family member's rare genetic condition has taken a toll physically, emotionally, and financially. It almost seems as though God answers every prayer they pray *except* the prayers they pray for their own family.

There have been moments when they've been tempted to throw in the prayer towel. But one promise has sustained them through the toughest times: "Blessed is the one who is not offended by me" (Luke 7:23 ESV).

Here's the context of this promise.

Jesus was doing miracles right and left. He was healing diseases, driving out demons, and restoring sight to the blind, but John the Baptist missed the miracle train. It seemed like Jesus was rescuing everybody except His most faithful follower, who was in prison. And John was His cousin! It seems that Jesus could have, and maybe should have, organized a rescue operation and busted John out before John was beheaded. Instead, Jesus sent a message via John's disciples. He told them to tell John about all the miracles Jesus was doing, and then He asked them to relay this promise: "Blessed is the one who is not offended by Me."

Have you ever felt that God was doing miracles for everyone and their brother, but you seem to be the odd one out? That God seems to be keeping His promises to everyone but you and your family? I wonder if that's how John the Baptist felt. And don't forget, he was family!

So what do you do when you feel as if God is answering everyone's prayers but yours? In the words of my friends, who have experienced their fair share of unanswered prayers: "We try to live our lives unoffended by God. Jesus promises blessings if we are not offended when He does things for others. And if He does it for them, He might do it for us. We don't know why God does what He does. We do know that 100 percent of the prayers we don't pray won't get answered."

I love this approach to prayer, this approach to life. It's the Circle Maker's mantra: "100 percent of the prayers I don't pray won't get answered."

Hyperlinked

One of the challenges John and Heidi have faced as they try to live unoffended by God involves their son. He was a normally developing toddler until one day when he suddenly and mysteriously lost all communication. They wondered if he would ever talk again. The fear of a wide variety of diagnoses, including high functioning autism, dropped them to their knees.

During those desperate days, they went to visit their pastor for counsel and encouragement. While he was praying for them, God gave him a promise. He jotted Isaiah 59:21 on a sticky note and handed it to them.

> "As for me, this is my covenant with them," says the LORD. "My Spirit, who is on you, will not depart from you, and my words that I have put in your mouth will always be on your lips, on the lips of your children and on the lips of their descendants—from this time on and forever," says the LORD.

The pastor shut his Bible and said, "I guess that settles it. Your child will talk."

For the past ten years, their prayers have been linked to that promise. In that moment, John and Heidi said, "a wall came crashing down" and "a promise came rushing in." It was the most naturally supernatural moment of their lives. Has it been clear sailing since then? No. Have they experienced disappointments? Yes. But that promise is circled in their Bible. They say, "God gave us a promise, and no matter how many times we have to keep circling, it's settled."

The other night Lora and I had dinner with John and Heidi. The highlight? When they told us their son brought home a 4.0 GPA on his most recent report card. I've been rejoicing ever since, and I absolutely believe that his academic performance is directly linked to the biblical promise his parents have circled for more than a decade.

Chapter 10

The 7th Circle: Passing On the Blessing

Nevertheless, for David's sake the LORD his God gave him a lamp in Jerusalem.

1 KINGS 15:4

David was a distant memory when this proclamation was made in 1 Kings 15:4. In fact, he'd been dead for eighty-six years. The epitaph on David's tombstone was fading, but David's legacy was alive and well. More than eight decades after the death of David, God established Asa, David's great-great-grandson, as the king of Judah. Why? *For David's sake.* David's influence was still tangible four generations later, and his legacy was the foundation upon which his descendants established their kingdoms.

That is our job as parents—to lay a strong foundation of faith that will secure God's blessing to the fourth generation. While we each need to position ourselves for God's blessing by obeying Him, I know that the blessings in my life were not paid for by me. My parents, grandparents, and great-grandparents made the down payment of prayer and faith before I was even born.

Far be it from me to put myself on par with King David, but I do believe that God will bless the fourth generation of Battersons *for Mark's sake*. And you can insert your name there too! I believe God wants to use our children in ways that we're not capable of even imagining. Their vision should be much larger and longer than ours simply because they stand on our shoulders. Every generation is called to position the next generation for greater things.

Autobiography

One of my grave concerns about American culture is that we celebrate fifteen minutes of fame more than a lifetime of faithfulness. We also know more about our favorite celebrities than we do our own ancestors. In fact, most of us know next to nothing about our great-great-grandparents. In many cases, we don't even know their names!

One of the ways I've tried to remedy that is by

writing books. I want my great-great-grandchildren to know exactly what I thought, what I prayed, and what I believed. And as long as my books stay in print, they'll have a window into my mind, my heart, and my soul. But even if you're not an author, I still believe that every parent owes his or her children an autobiography. It might only be a *Reader's Digest* version, but you owe it to your descendants to put your testimony on paper. And if you can't write a book, write a letter.

John Quincy Adams, our sixth president, did just that. Adams was more than a distinguished statesman; he was a committed follower of Christ. George Washington said that, as an ambassador, Adams was "the most valuable public character we have abroad."[12] In addition to serving as secretary of state under James Monroe, John Quincy Adams is the only president to have served in Congress *before* and *after* his presidency. What most Americans don't know is that Adams was an avid student of Scripture: he made it his practice to read through the entire Bible once every year. During his tenure as a diplomat overseas, Adams became concerned that his youngest son, Charles Francis Adams, should learn how to study the Bible. As a result, he wrote nine letters between 1811 and 1813 teaching Charles how to study the Bible. Those letters were actually published in book form in 1848.

Lora and I certainly want to leave a monetary inheritance for our children, but more than that, we want to leave a spiritual blessing. While it's not easy to define, I believe a generational blessing is the favor that falls to our children because of our faith. If children aren't walking in faith, the full blessing is nullified. But if they choose to follow in the footsteps of their father's faith, the blessing will follow them their entire lives. And it will always be greater than the sum total of their obedience. The blessings of God don't add up. They multiply!

The Prototype

While the Bible doesn't give us a formula for blessing our children, the baptism of Jesus is a great microcosm. Those who witnessed His baptism heard the voice of the heavenly Father say, "This is my beloved Son, in whom I am well pleased" (Matthew 17:5 KJV).

I know this could come across as heretical, but Jesus hadn't done much up to this point in His life—and He was thirty! No miracles. No parables. And that's what I love about this commendation: the Father celebrates a small act of obedience. And while we start out that way as parents, celebrating our kids' baby steps, we too often raise our expectations to an unattainable level. Or we make the mistake of basing our blessing on behavior alone.

I have three primary goals as a father.

First, I want my kids to know that *I love them no matter what*. And nothing they do can change that. Our heavenly Father's love is unconditional, and that means we can't do anything to make God love us any more or any less. God loves us perfectly. And while we're not capable of unconditional love, that is the standard the heavenly Father has set for us. The blessing is not behavioral; it's relational.

Second, I want my kids to know that *I am well pleased with them*. That doesn't mean that we make our kids the center of our universe. But our kids need to know that they make us proud, make us smile, and make us laugh.

Third, I want my kids to know that *I am there for them*. That means answering my cell phone whenever they call for whatever reason. That means chauffeuring when I don't feel like it. That means getting up early to have devotions or staying up late when they are out past curfew.

The Generational Blessing

Jacob was far from the model dad. After all, his favoritism toward Joseph was so pronounced that the other siblings faked his death. Can you say *dysfunctional*? I'm pretty sure a few television networks would have been vying for the rights to their reality show!

Yet despite the multitude of mistakes he made as

a father, Jacob finished strong as a grandfather. And that's the quintessence of being a grandparent: it's a second chance to get it right. At the end of his life, Jacob spoke a prophetic word over each of his children. Actually, some of them seemed like curses! He called one of them a viper and another a ravenous wolf. But that is what they were; these were the same sons who had sold their brother into slavery. A generational blessing doesn't negate character flaws. In fact, character is the combination that unlocks the blessings of God. The more character your kids have, the more God can bless them because they have a foundation to sustain it.

While some of the ancient blessings that Jacob pronounced are difficult to understand, they set a precedent for parents. And the blessing of Joseph, in particular, is a prototype. I believe our children's greatest subconscious longing is for the full blessing of their parents. Without it, children live with an ambiguous feeling of incompleteness.

Genesis 49:22–26 (ESV) records the generational blessing of Joseph:

Joseph is a fruitful bough,
    a fruitful bough by a spring;
    his branches run over the wall.
The archers bitterly attacked him,
    shot at him, and harassed him severely,
yet his bow remained unmoved;
    his arms were made agile
by the hands of the Mighty one of Jacob . . .
by the God of your father who will help you,
    by the Almighty who will bless you
    with blessings of heaven above,
blessings of the deep that crouches beneath,
    blessings of the breasts and the womb.
The blessings of your father
    are mighty beyond the blessings of my parents,
    up to the bounties of the everlasting hills.
May they be on the head of Joseph,
    and on the brow of him who was set apart
        from his brothers.

Generational blessing is something that can only be passed from parents to children. It's not just a singular event, like the dubbing of knighthood. The blessing is conveyed day in and day out, from birth to death.

But there are defining moments along the way, like the final blessing and testament of Jacob. At critical junctures, parental blessings bridge the gap between stages of life. When children become teenagers, graduate from high school, or get married, those are watershed moments. Parents need to step up and step in with a blessing. The blessing is more than tacit approval or an occasional pat on the back. It is the conveyance of spiritual authority. It's an expression of our faith in our children. The blessing is the way we get in their corner and back them up spiritually. Will they make mistakes? Absolutely. Will they mishandle some of the opportunities we hand off? No doubt. But children need to learn the same way we did—by making mistakes. If they continue to make the same mistake over and over again, parental intervention is in order. But children need to learn how to let God pick them up and dust them off. They need to learn how to lay hold of the blessings of God with their own two hands.

Memorial Offerings

Acts 10 spotlights one of the most significant turning points in church history. Until that point, Christianity was a sect of Judaism. The first Gentile convert was a centurion in the Italian Regiment named Cornelius. And one byline reveals everything I need to know about Cornelius: he "prayed to God regularly" (v. 2). When you pray to God regularly, irregular things will happen on a regular basis. And that is precisely what happened. A double vision led to a divine appointment that resulted in the salvation of Cornelius and his household. And the door of salvation was opened to anyone and everyone. If you are a Gentile, you can trace your spiritual genealogy back to Cornelius. If he hadn't been saved, you wouldn't be saved.

Now let me backtrack to one profound statement in Acts 10:4 (ESV):

Your prayers and your alms have ascended as a memorial before God.

We have a tendency to forget what we've prayed for, but God never forgets. Every prayer is a memorial offering. And just like the memorials that dot the nation's capital, our prayers are Lincoln Memorials and Washington Monuments to God. Just like the prayers of my grandfather that have stalked me my entire life, the blessings of God trail us our entire lives, and those blessings have a long tail. The warranty doesn't lapse after the fourth generation. According to the promise of Exodus 20:6, God's blessings are guaranteed to a thousand generations.

Sometimes the blessings we inherit are not the derivative of anything we've done. They are the spin-off of someone else's faithfulness generations ago. And their faithfulness nets blessings decades after they have died. I've come to realize that my destiny is inextricably linked to my parents' and my grandparents' legacy. And my legacy will influence the destiny of my children, my grandchildren, and my great-grandchildren.

I realize that might be a scary thought for some of you, given what your family has been like. But it doesn't need to cause you to feel anxious. If you are a child of God, all generational curses are broken. You don't have to make the same mistakes your parents made. And for the record, Asa didn't. Unlike his father but just like his great-great-grandfather David, Asa did what was right in the eyes of the Lord.

Each of us inherits a legacy from our ancestors: it is part of our birthright. And each of us leaves a legacy for our progeny: it is part of the inheritance we leave behind for them. David served God's purpose in his own generation, but he did more than that. He also left a legacy for generations to come.

A Thousand Generations

Jacob did a lot of things wrong, but he got one thing right: he pronounced a blessing on his children. And the results speak for themselves. In an 1899 article in *Harper's* magazine, the inimitable Mark Twain summed it up best:

If the statistics are right, the Jews constitute but one percent of the human race. It suggests a nebulous dim puff of stardust lost in the blaze of the Milky Way. Properly the Jew ought hardly to be heard of, but he is heard of, has always been heard of. He is as prominent on the planet as any other people, and his commercial importance is extravagantly out of proportion to the smallness of his bulk. His contributions to the world's list of great names in literature, science, art, music, finance, medicine, and abstruse learning are also way out of proportion to the weakness of his numbers. He has made a marvelous fight in the world, in all the ages; and has done it with his hands tied behind him. He could be vain of himself, and be excused for it. The Egyptian, the Babylonian, and the Persian rose, filled the planet with sound and splendor, then faded to dream-stuff and passed away; the Greek and the Roman followed, and made a vast noise, and they are gone; other peoples have sprung up and held their torch high for a time, but it burned out, and they sit in twilight now, or have vanished. The Jew saw them all, beat them all, and is now what he always was, exhibiting no decadence, no infirmities of age, no weakening of his parts, no slowing of his energies, no dulling of his alert and aggressive mind. All things are mortal but the Jew; all other forces pass, but he remains. What is the secret of his immortality?[13]

Twain asked the question, "What is the secret?" If you reverse engineer it, I honestly believe that the only explanation is a blessing that traces all the way back to Abraham, Isaac, and Jacob.

A Heart for Missions

My father-in-law, Bob Schmidgall, had the biggest heart for missions of anybody I've ever known. He pastored Calvary Church in Naperville, Illinois, for more than thirty years. And while he influenced that city in profound ways, his influence was felt around the world. For many years, Calvary Church was the leading missions-giving church in its denomination of ten-thousand-plus churches.

Because that is what his life was about, it seemed to us that is what his death should be about too. So those who attended his funeral were encouraged to give a gift to missions in lieu of flowers. Then, more than a year after his funeral, our entire family flew to Ethiopia to visit a church my father-in-law had helped to establish years before. We presented the pastor of that church, Betta Mengistu, with the monies that had been donated at the funeral. That moment was one of the defining moments of my life. It dawned on me that here we were, more than a year after my father-in-law's death, and he was still giving to missions! His destiny had become his legacy. And that legacy goes beyond finances.

Joel Schmidgall, our executive pastor and my brother-in-law, is living out his father's legacy. He has his father's enlarged heart for missions, and he has championed missions at National Community Church. We took twenty-five mission trips last year, and we dream of the day when we're taking fifty-two trips. We also gave more than $1 million to missions last year. And our strategic plan for the future, called our 2020 Vision, is to double that number so we're giving $2 million to missions annually.

That is our destiny as a church, but it is also our legacy as a family. And that legacy is our destiny.

Daddy Warbucks

In Malachi 3:9–12, the Lord said,

> You are under a curse—your whole nation—because you are robbing me. Bring the whole tithe into the storehouse, that there may be food in my house. Test me in this . . . and see if I will not throw open the floodgates of heaven and pour out so much blessing that there will not be room enough to store it. I will prevent pests from devouring your crops, and the vines in your fields will not drop their fruit before it is ripe. . . . Then all nations will call you blessed.

This passage reveals the heart of God. God wants to bless you beyond your ability to contain it, but like any good parent, He won't bless you beyond your ability to steward it. If you don't have the maturity to be a wise steward of the blessing, that blessing actually turns into a curse.

When our kids were young, we often took them to Chuck E. Cheese's for their birthdays. Kids can run wild and play games while catatonic parents sit and stare. For whatever reason, I asked Parker how many tokens he wanted for his birthday. I was expecting a triple-digit number, but Parker said, "Five." I couldn't believe he asked for so few. I wasn't sure if he thought I was poor or stingy, but I decided to lead him into the blessing because Daddy Warbucks can do way better than five tokens! I said, "Parker, do you want five or six tokens?" He said, "Six." I said, "Do you want six or seven?" He said, "Seven." I said, "Do you want seven or eight?" He said, "Eight." I kept working him up until we got to ten. When I asked, "Do you want ten or eleven?" Parker said, "Ten."

I have no idea why he stopped at ten. Maybe he just ran out of fingers to count on. But I could have and would have given him eleven tokens, but his ability to *be blessed* was less than my ability *to bless*. God is always trying to lead us to the place of greater blessing. He wants to give us what we don't deserve. He wants to bless us beyond our ability to contain it, but most of us can't envision more than ten tokens!

So, how do we experience the blessing of God?

The key is living in obedience to Him. And one aspect of obedience is living in a way that puts no limits on God's ability to bless us. When we sin, we limit God's ability to bless us. The same is true of selfishness. He loves us too much to spoil us. But if you cultivate a humble and grateful spirit, God will bless you. And as long as you realize that God blesses you to be a blessing, He'll continue to open the flood-gates of heaven.

Family Tree

Few Americans have shaped our country the way Jonathan Edwards did. He was more than a theological genius—entering Yale at the age of twelve and eventually serving as president of Princeton University until his death in 1758. And he was more than the author of dozens of books. Edwards was also a committed father of three sons and eight daughters.

In 1900, A. E. Winsup researched Edwards' family tree. Among his known descendants are 300 preachers, 100 lawyers, 65 professors, 56 doctors, 30 judges, 13 authors, 13 college presidents, 3 US senators, and 1 vice president.

Every night that Edwards was home with his family, he spent an hour with his children. He'd sit in his favorite chair and converse with them. Then he'd pray a blessing over them every night. The legacy Edwards left to his lineage was not the result of luck. It was layer upon layer of blessing. It started with his personal devotion to God, and that is where the blessing always begins. Your devotion to God will lay a foundation and set a standard for your children to build on.

On January 12, 1723, Jonathan Edwards made a written dedication of himself to God. He wrote out his pledge in his diary and revisited it often over the years.

> I made a solemn dedication of myself to God, and wrote it down; giving up myself, and all that I had to God; to be for the future, in no respect, my own; to act as one that had no right to himself, in any respect. And solemnly vowed, to take God for my whole portion and felicity; looking on nothing else, as any part of my happiness, nor acting as if it were.[14]

Chapter 11

Teachable Moments

*You must commit yourselves wholeheartedly
to these commands that I am giving you
today. Repeat them again and again to your
children. Talk about them when you are at
home and when you are on the road, when you
are going to bed and when you are getting up.*

Deuteronomy 6:6–7 nlt

I n his memoir *A Touch of Wonder*, Arthur Gordon shares one of the defining moments of his childhood. When he was a small boy, his family spent their summers at a seaside cottage. Late one night, after Arthur had fallen asleep, his father came into his room, picked him up out of bed, and carried him down to the beach. Then he told Arthur to look up into the night sky and watch. Just as his father said that, a shooting star streaked across the sky. Then another. And another. His father explained that on certain nights in August, the sky would put on its own fireworks display. Six decades later, that evening ranks as one of Arthur Gordon's happiest remembrances.

Reflecting on the influence of his father, Gordon said that his dad believed that a new experience was more important for a small boy than an unbroken night of sleep. In Gordon's words, "I had the usual quota of playthings, but these are forgotten now. What I remember is the night the stars fell, the day we rode in a caboose, the time we tried to skin the alligator, the telegraph we made that really worked."[15]

What will your kids remember from their childhood?

I'll give you a hint: it won't be the things you purchased for them. It will be the things you did with them. But it probably won't be the things you preplanned as a parent. It will be the improvised moments that can only be prompted by a parent's sixth sense. If you capitalize on those moments, you'll make the same kind of impression on your kids that Arthur Gordon's father did on him.

Half of parenting is putting together a great game plan.

The other half is making the most of teachable moments.

Arthur Gordon captured the essence of his father's ability to make memories this way:

"My Father had, to a marvelous degree, the gift of opening doors for his children, of leading them into areas of splendid newness. This, surely, is the most valuable legacy we can pass on to the next generation: not money, not houses or heirlooms, but a capacity for wonder and gratitude, a sense of aliveness and joy."[16]

I want to be the kind of dad who opens doors for my kids. I want to feed their curiosity and spark their sense of adventure. And I'm convinced that the key to all of the above is prayer.

The Rhythm of Parenting

The centerpiece of the Jewish Torah is the Shema. It begins,

Hear, O Israel: The LORD our God, the LORD is one. Love the LORD your God with all your heart and with all your soul and with all your strength. (Deuteronomy 6:4–5)

Whenever I do a baby dedication at National Community Church, I always pray that the child will grow up to love God with all of their heart and soul and mind and strength. Jesus reduced the entire law to this one Great Commandment. As parents, we want our kids to be great at sports or great at math or great at music. But if my kids are going to be great at anything, I want them to be great at obeying the Great Commandment (Matthew 22:37–38). That is true greatness.

Then the Shema shifts the focus to parents:

And you must commit yourselves wholeheartedly to these commands that I am giving you today. Repeat them again and again to your children. Talk about them when you are at home and when you are on the road, when you are going to bed and when you are getting up. Tie them to your hands and wear them on your forehead as reminders. Write them on the doorposts of your house and on your gates. (Deuteronomy 6:6–9 NLT)

Sometimes the obvious eludes us, so let me state it as succinctly as I can: in Judaism, *the parent is the priest* and *the home is the temple*. If we miss that, we're off center.

What I love most about the Shema is the way it tunes itself to the rhythm of life. Every time a Jewish person walked in or out of their home, they walked past the mezuzah—a small box containing a piece of parchment with the twenty-two lines of the Shema written on it. It was a ritual reminder of the Great Commandment. As parents, we need to add mezuzahs to our children's world. That might mean texting them a daily scripture or praying with them at the dinner table. But the key to cultivating a prayer life is playing off the natural rhythms of life. Of course, eating and sleeping are major cues for us. When your kids get older, curfew will be another one. Instead of staying up and worrying about your kids, use that window of time to pray for them.

My friends Josh and Justin Mayo have amazing parents. Sam and Jeanne Mayo have impacted thousands of lives, but none more than their own sons. Justin told me that when he was a teen, some of the most significant conversations he had with his parents happened after curfew! The fact that his parents were always waiting for him didn't just keep him accountable; it demonstrated that they were there for them. And they didn't pull out the Breathalyzer every time their kids came home late. That doesn't mean you close your eyes to something you need to confront, but the key is to be there for them when they are most vulnerable.

Identifying teachable moments starts with capitalizing on the times when your kids are a *captive audience.* One of the most obvious is when you are tucking them into bed. Bedtime and mealtime are two great opportunities to leverage. I've also found that chauffeuring my kids all over tarnation is a great way to spend quality time with them. And family vacations, if you are able to take them, are another great window of opportunity.

Make-or-Break Moments

Discerning teachable moments is one of the fine arts of parenting. When your child strikes out or gets bullied at school or has their first crush on a classmate, it's an opportunity to be a crash pad or sounding board. But before you wax eloquent with words of wisdom, just listen to what your children have to say.

The context will certainly change as your kids get older. You'll undoubtedly read some texts and e-mails that you wish you hadn't. You'll discover some inside information about a party they were at, find a condom hidden in their closet, or find out that they didn't go where they said they were going and weren't with the person they said they were with. Before you lose your temper, realize that these are teachable moments. They are also make-or-break moments as parents. And prayer is the key to discerning them.

At the base of your brainstem lies a cluster of nerve cells called the reticular activating system (RAS). We are constantly bombarded by countless stimuli vying for our attention, and it is the job of the RAS to determine what gets noticed and what goes unnoticed. Like a mental radar system, the RAS determines what makes a blip.

The RAS is one reason why goal setting is so important. It creates a category in your RAS, and you start noticing anything and everything that will help you accomplish the goal. Prayer is important for the same reason. It sanctifies your RAS so you notice what God wants you to notice. The more you pray, the more you notice. It's no coincidence that being *watchful* and *prayerful* are coupled together in Colossians 4:2. The word *watchful* is a throwback to the ancient watchmen whose job it was to sit on the city walls and scan the horizon for attacking armies or trading caravans. They saw sooner and farther than anyone else. Prayer opens our spiritual eyes so we see sooner and see further.

Parents are watchmen and watchwomen. If you want to spot teachable moments, the key is watching and praying. Prayer primes us as parents. It helps us see and seize teachable moments that can become defining moments in our children's lives.

Chapter 12

Holy Complications

Children are a gift from the Lord;
they are a reward from him.
Children born to a young man
are like arrows in a warrior's hands.

PSALM 127:3–4 NLT

One reason many people get frustrated spiritually is that they believe it should get easier to do the will of God. I don't know if my thoughts here will be encouraging or discouraging, but the will of God doesn't get easier; it gets harder. It doesn't get less complicated; it gets more complicated. But I believe these complications are evidence of God's blessing. And since a complication is from God, it's a holy complication.

You need to come to terms with this two-sided truth: *the blessings of God won't just bless you; they will also complicate your life.* Sin will complicate your life in negative ways, in ways it should not be complicated. The blessings of God will complicate your life in positive ways, in ways it should be complicated.

When Lora and I got married, it complicated our lives. Praise God for complications! We have three complications named Parker, Summer, and Josiah.

I can't imagine my life without these complications. With every promotion come complications. As you earn more income, your taxes become more complicated. My point? Blessings will complicate your life, but they will complicate your life in the way God wants.

So my prayer for myself—and for you—is this: "Lord, complicate our lives!"

Sleepless Nights

Some of the longest nights of my life were the sleepless nights when Parker was a baby. He had a bad case of colic that caused him to cry incessantly for no discernible reason. The joy of having our first child was quickly displaced by sleep deprivation. The only thing that calmed Parker was running the bathtub faucet. I remember going into the bathroom, turning on the water, and holding Parker for hours on end. Our water bill was so uncharacteristically high that the water company actually thought there had been some kind of mistake. Nope. Just a crying baby!

When you're holding a baby who won't stop crying, you can't stop praying. It's all we knew to do. Parker must be one of the most prayed-for babies in his generation. But that's the reason I'm grateful for his colic. That's the reason I believe God will use Parker in great ways. Lora and I wrapped our arms around him and prayed circles around him every time he cried. Those were some long nights and long prayers, but now that we're seeing these prayers answered in his life as a teenager, we wouldn't trade those sleepless nights for anything in the world.

When we get discouraged as parents, we have to remember the power of a single prayer. One prayer can change anything. One prayer can change everything. This I know from personal experience.

On Call

Our family started attending Calvary Church when I was in the eighth grade. It was already a megachurch with thousands of members, but my father-in-law, who was the pastor there, had an amazing memory for names and faces. If he met you once, he would remember your name forever. Despite the size of the church, he had a hospitable spirit that gave him an air of accessibility. Maybe that's why my parents felt like they could call him at two o'clock in the morning after my doctor issued a code blue and half a dozen nurses came rushing into my ICU room. I thought I was taking my last breath.

My mom stayed by my side while my dad called information and got a home phone number for the Schmidgalls. In less than ten minutes, my future father-in-law was at my bedside in his black double-breasted Superman suit that I would later swear he slept in.

Bob Schmidgall was a large man with large hands. They looked more like meat hooks than hands. When he prayed for someone, his hands would envelop that person's head like a skullcap. When he laid his hands on my head, I remember thinking, *There is no way God isn't going to answer his prayer.*

He had a familiarity with God that was disarming. He had a faith in God that was reassuring.

He could have called a staff member to make the visit; he didn't. He could have waited until morning; he didn't. He sacrificed a full night's sleep to pray for a thirteen-year-old kid who was fighting for his life.

Little did he know that this thirteen-year-old kid would one day marry his daughter, Lora. Little did he know that this thirteen-year-old kid would one day give him his first grandchild, a colicky baby boy named Parker. There is no way he could have ever known, but that is the glorious mystery of prayer.

You never completely know who you are praying for and who is praying for you. You never know *how* or *when* God will answer your prayers. But you can be sure of this: *your prayers will shape the destiny of your family for generations to come.* And if you are willing to interrupt your sleep cycle, if you are willing to get on your knees and intercede for your family, God will answer your prayers long after you are long gone.

Don't lose heart.
Don't lose hope.
Don't lose faith.
Keep circling!

The Power of a Seed

Toward the end of his life, Honi the Circle Maker was walking down a dirt road when he saw a man planting a carob tree. Honi questioned him, "How long will it take this tree to bear fruit?" The man replied, "Seventy years." Honi said, "Are you quite sure you will live another seventy years to eat its fruit?" The man replied, "Perhaps not. However, when I was born into this world, I found many carob trees planted by my father and grandfather. Just as they planted trees for me, I am planting trees for my children and grandchildren so they will be able to eat the fruit of these trees."

This incident changed the way Honi prayed. In a moment of revelation, the Circle Maker realized that praying is planting. Each prayer is like a seed that gets planted in the ground. It disappears for a season, but it eventually bears fruit that blesses future generations. In fact, our prayers bear fruit forever. Even when we die, our prayers don't. Each prayer takes on a life—an eternal life—of its own.

Because we are surrounded by technology that makes our lives faster and easier, we tend to think about spiritual realities in technological terms. We want to reap the very second we sow. We want God to microwave answers, MapQuest directions, and Twitter instructions. We want things to happen at the speed of light instead of the speed of a seed planted in the ground, but almost all spiritual realities in Scripture are described in agricultural terms. We want our prayers to be answered immediately, but that isn't the way it works in God's kingdom.

Your kids are carob trees that will bear fruit seventy years from now. As parents, we need the patience of the planter, the oversight of the farmer, and the mind-set of the sower.

Notes

1. Harley Rotbart, "Just Parent, No Philosphy Required", The New York Times (April 18, 2012), http://parenting.blogs.nytimes.com/2012/04/18 /just-parent-no-philosophy-required/.
2. "Preparing a Place to Pray," http://anchoryourlife .com/prayer/place.htm, accessed December 24, 2013.
3. To connect with the Johnsons or to track what God is doing in Connor's life, visit their website at www .connormoments.com, accessed March 15, 2012.
4. Laurie Beth Jones, *The Power of Positive Prophecy: Finding the Hidden Potential in Everyday Life* (New York: Hyperion, 1999), ix.

5. Frederick Buechner, *The Alphabet of Grace* (San Francisco: HarperOne, 2009), 14.

6. Ibid.

7. Paco Underhill, *Why We Buy: The Science of Shopping*, rev. ed. (New York: Simon and Schuster, 2008), 111.

8. Jack Handey, *Deeper Thoughts: All New, All Crispy* (New York: Hyperion, 1993), 3.

9. Frederick Buechner, *Secrets in the Dark: A Life in Sermons* (San Francisco: HarperOne, 2006), 40.

10. Lisa Bevere, *Girls with Swords: How to Carry Your Cross Like a Hero* (Colorado Springs: WaterBrook, 2013), 7.

11. Julianne Holt-Lunstad, Wendy A. Birmingham, and Kathleen C. Light, "Influence of a 'Warm Touch' Support Enhancement Intervention Among Married Couples on Ambulatory Blood Pressure, Oxytocin, Alpha-Amylase, and Cortisol," *Psychosomatic Medicine* 70 (2008): 976–85.

12. Don Hawkinson, *Character for Life: An American Heritage: Profiles of Great Men and Women of Faith Who Shaped Western Civilization* (Green Forest, AR: New Leaf Publishing Group, 2005), 89.

13. "10 Great Jewish and Israeli Quotes," *The Algemeiner*, http://www.algemeiner.com/2012/04/26/10-great-jewish-and-israeli-quotes/, accessed December, 29 2013.

14. Jonathan Edwards, *A Treatise Concerning Religious Affections in Three Parts* (New Haven, CT: Yale University, 1959), xxvii.
15. Arthur Gordon, *A Touch of Wonder: Staying in Love with Life* (New York: Jove, 1996).
16. Ibid.

Bible Versions Cited

Scripture quotations marked NLT are taken from the *Holy Bible*, New Living Translation, copyright © 1996. Used by permission of Tyndale House Publishers, Inc., Wheaton, Illinois 60189. All rights reserved.

Scripture quotations marked TLB are taken from *The Living Bible*. Copyright © 1971 by Tyndale House Publishers, Inc., Wheaton, Illinois 60189. All rights reserved.

Prayers and Reflections

_____

_____

_____

_____

_____

_____

_____

_____

_____

_____

_____

_____

_____

_____

_____

_____

Prayers and Reflections

_____

_____

_____

_____

_____

_____

_____

_____

_____

_____

_____

_____

_____

_____

_____

_____

_____

_____

Prayers and Reflections

_____

_____

_____

_____

_____

_____

_____

_____

_____

_____

_____

_____

_____

_____

_____

_____

_____

Prayers and Reflections

_____

_____

_____

_____

_____

_____

_____

_____

_____

_____

_____

_____

_____

_____

_____

_____

_____

Prayers and Reflections

_____

_____

_____

_____

_____

_____

_____

_____

_____

_____

_____

_____

_____

_____

_____

_____

Prayers and Reflections

_____

_____

_____

_____

_____

_____

_____

_____

_____

_____

_____

_____

_____

_____

_____

_____

_____

Prayers and Reflections

_____

_____

_____

_____

_____

_____

_____

_____

_____

_____

_____

_____

_____

_____

_____

_____

_____

Prayers and Reflections

_____

_____

_____

_____

_____

_____

_____

_____

_____

_____

_____

_____

_____

_____

_____

_____

Prayers and Reflections

_____

_____

_____

_____

_____

_____

_____

_____

_____

_____

_____

_____

_____

_____

_____

_____

All In

You Are One Decision Away From a
Totally Different Life

Mark Batterson,
New York Times Bestselling author

The Gospel costs nothing. You can't earn it or buy
it. It can only be received as a free gift compliments
of God's grace. It doesn't cost anything, but it demands everything. It demands that we go "all in,"
a term that simply means placing all that you have
into God's hands. Pushing it all in. And that's where
we get stuck—spiritual no man's land. We're afraid that if we go all in that we might
miss out on what this life has to offer. It's not true. The only thing you'll miss out on is
everything God has to offer. And the good news is this: if you don't hold out on God,
God won't hold out on you. Readers will find Batterson's writing filled with his cus-
tomary vivid, contemporary illustrations as well as biblical characters like Shamgar
and Elisha and Jonathan and . . . Judas.

No one has ever sacrificed anything for God. If you always get back more than you gave
up, have you sacrificed anything at all? The eternal reward always outweighs the temporal sacrifice. At the end of the day, our greatest regret will be whatever we didn't give
back to God. What we didn't push back across the table to Him. Eternity will reveal that
holding out is losing out.

The message of All In is simple: if Jesus is not Lord of all then Jesus is not Lord at all.
It's all or nothing. It's now or never. Kneeling at the foot of cross of Christ and surren-
dering to His Lordship is a radical act of dethroning yourself and enthroning Christ
as King. It's also an act of disowning yourself. Nothing belongs to you. Not even you.

Batterson writes,for many years, I thought I was following Jesus. I wasn't. I had invited Jesus to follow me. I call it inverted Christianity. And it's a subtle form of selfishness that masquerades as spirituality. That's when I sold out and bought in. When did
we start believing that the gospel is an insurance plan? It's a daring plan. Jesus did
not die just to keep us safe. He died to make us dangerous."

Hardcover, Jacketed: 978-0-310-33305-0

All In, Student Edition

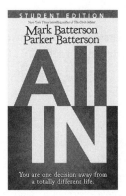

Mark Batterson
with Parker Batterson

Halfway is no way to live.

Quit holding back. Quit holding out.

It's time to go all in and all out for God.

The good news is this: If you don't hold out on God, God won't hold out on you. If you give everything you have to follow Jesus, you'll receive amazing spiritual rewards. But this reality also comes with a deeper truth: Nothing belongs to you. Not even you.

In *All In: Student Edition*, Mark and Parker Batterson explore what going all in can mean for your life, sharing unique illustrations and unforgettable stories, as well as compelling accounts of biblical characters. Throughout, they demonstrate the amazing things that can happen when you surrender to the Lordship of Jesus Christ.

Mark Batterson writes: "When did we start believing that God wants to send us to safe places to do easy things? Jesus didn't die to keep us safe. He died to make us dangerous."

Available in stores and online!

The Circle Maker

Praying Circles Around Your
Biggest Dreams and Greatest Fears

Mark Batterson

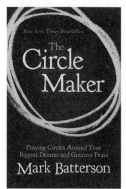

According to Pastor Mark Batterson in
his book, The Circle Maker, "Drawing
prayer circles around our dreams isn't
just a mechanism whereby we accomplish great things for God. It's a
mechanism whereby God accomplishes great things in us."

Do you ever sense that there's far more to prayer, and to God's
vision for your life, than what you're experiencing? It's time you
learned from the legend of Honi the Circle Maker—a man bold
enough to draw a circle in the sand and not budge from inside it
until God answered his prayers for his people.

What impossibly big dream is God calling you to draw a prayer
circle around? Sharing inspiring stories from his own experiences
as a circle maker, Mark Batterson will help you uncover your heart's
deepest desires and God-given dreams and unleash them through
the kind of audacious prayer that God delights to answer.

Hardcover, Printed: 978-0-310-33302-9

Available in stores and online!

The Circle Maker, Student Edition

Dream Big, Pray Hard, Think Long

Mark Batterson
with Parker Batterson

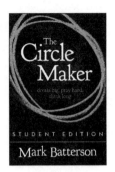

Prayer can sometimes be a frightening thing. How do you approach the Maker of the world, and what exactly can you pray for? In this student adaptation of *The Circle Maker*, Pastor Mark Batterson uses the true legend of Honi the circle maker, a first-century Jewish sage whose bold prayer saved a generation, to uncover the boldness God asks of us at times, and to unpack what powerful prayer can mean in your life. Drawing inspiration from his own experiences as a circle maker, as well as sharing stories of young people who have experienced God's blessings, Batterson explores how you can approach God in a new way by drawing prayer circles around your dreams, your problems, and, most importantly, God's promises. In the process, you'll discover this simple yet life-changing truth:

> God honors bold prayers and bold prayers honor God.

And you're never too young for God to use you for amazing things.

Available in stores and online!

Draw the Circle

To 40 Day Prayer Challenge

Mark Batterson

Do you pray as often and as boldly as you want to? There is a way to experience a deeper, more passionate, persistent, and intimate prayer life.

Drawing from forty days of true stories, Mark Batterson applies the principles of his New York Times bestselling book The Circle Maker to teach us a new way to pray. As thousands of readers quickly became many tens of thousands, true stories of miraculous and inspiring answers to prayer began to pour in, and as those stories were shared, others were bolstered in their faith to pray with even more boldness.

In Draw the Circle, through forty true, faith-building stories of God's answers to prayer, daily scriptures and prayer prompts, Batterson inspires you to pray and keep praying like never before. Begin a lifetime of watching God work. Believe in the God who can do all things. Experience the power of bold prayer and even bolder faith in Draw the Circle.

Softcover: 978-0-310-32712-7

The Circle Maker Prayer Journal

Mark Batterson

Discover the power of bold prayer and even bolder faith in God's promises. Based on Mark Batterson's revolutionary, bestselling book on prayer, The Circle Maker Prayer Journal features inspirational sayings and plenty of space to record your prayers, God's answers, and spiritual insights. Learn to pray powerful words according to God's will—and see the amazing results! Gather your prayers so you can go back and see how God has been answering since you started your amazing prayer journey.

The Circle Maker Prayer Journal will be your guide to making your life goals a reality of answered prayers instead of just fleeting wishes. This handsomely bound keepsake volume will become your written record for dreaming big and seeing God answer.

Italian Duo-Tone™, Brown: 978-0-310-32834-6

Praying Circles around Your Children

Mark Batterson

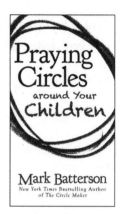

Mark Batterson shares a perfect blend of biblical yet practical advice that will revolutionize your prayer life by giving you a new vocabulary and a new methodology. You'll see how prayer is your secret weapon. Through stories of parents just like you, Batterson shares five prayer circles that will not only help you pray for your kids, but also pray through your kids.

Batterson teaches about how to create prayer lists unique to your family, claim God-inspired promises for your children, turn your family circle into a prayer circle, and discover your child's life themes. And he not only tells you how, he illustrates why.

As Batterson says, "I realize that not everyone inherited a prayer legacy like I did, but you can leave a legacy for generations to come. Your prayers have the power to shape the destiny of your children and your children's children. It's time to start circling."

Booklet: 978-0-310-32550-5

Available in stores and online!

The Circle Maker for Kids

One Prayer Can
Change Everything

Mark Batterson

"One prayer can change everything."

A terrible drought had hit the land. Gardens died, rivers ran dry; the Israelites had one last hope: Honi the Rainmaker. So they called upon him to pray, and Honi did something strange ... something bold.

Would God send the rains and save the people?

Basing this story on his adult bestseller *The Circle Maker*, Mark Batterson shares the ancient Jewish legend of Honi the Rainmaker with children to teach them about the power of prayer.

Available in stores and online!

ZONDERVAN®
.com